THE FRAGILE MALE

THE FRAGILE MALE

Ben Greenstein

A BIRCH LANE PRESS BOOK
Published by Carol Publishing Group

8-17-95

For Lorraine, Adam and Saul

First Carol Publishing Group edition 1994

Copyright © 1993 by Ben Greenstein

A Birch Lane Press Book
Published by Carol Publishing Group
Birch Lane Press is a registered trademark of Carol Communications Group
Editorial Offices: 600 Madison Avenue, New York, N.Y. 10022
Sales and Distribution Offices: 120 Enterprise Avenue, Secaucus, N.J. 07094
In Canada: Canadian Manda Group, P.O. Box 920, Station U, Toronto,
   Ontario M8Z 5P9
Queries regarding rights and permissions should be addressed to
Carol Publishing Group, 600 Madison Avenue, New York, N.Y. 10022

First published in Great Britain in 1993 by Boxtree Limited

Carol Publishing books are available at special
discounts for bulk purchases, for sales promotions, fund-raising, or
educational purposes. Special editions can be created to
specifications. For details, contact Special Sales Department, Carol
Publishing Group, 120 Enterprise Avenue, Secaucus, N.J. 07094

Manufactured in the United States of America
10 9 8 7 6 5 4 3 2 1

Library of Congress Cataloging-in Publication Data

Greenstein, Ben, 1941-
    The fragile male : the decline of a redundant species / by Ben
Greenstein.
       p.   cm.
    "A Birch Lane Press book."
    ISBN 1-55972-245-2
    1. Man—Psychology. 2. Man—Attitudes. 3. Human behavior.
4. Hormones. I. Title.
HQ1090.G76   1994
155.3'32—dc20
                                              94-16679
                                              CIP

Contents

Preface

In Dillons booksellers in London there is a selection headed Gender Studies, and virtually all the books have been written by women about women and what they have endured at the hands of men. This book should help to increase the pitifully small collection of those written by men about men. That, however, is not why it was written. During my research on brain sexual differentiation I began to think less about rats and more about men. Initially I was intrigued by the evidence that the brain is intrinsically female, and becomes male only through the intervention of the male sex hormone testosterone. This prompted the speculation that originally there were only females until one started budding off males for a specific set of purposes. These were, principally, to feed, guard and inseminate the female. From my reading it became clear that for most species, and certainly in the case of humans, something went terribly wrong and the female lost control of the male. He became not a guardian but a biologically programmed tyrant. In fact, if the male's tyrant status is removed it is positively bad for his health. It is but a short step from there to the modern human male, who is rapidly losing his traditional status, and all other questions pall beside that which asks how he will respond to the deletion of his *raison d'être*.

It was that question which fuelled the engine in me that kicked this book into life. And when I started reading I realized that precious little is known about the human male, and certainly not enough to answer the question.

Therefore I completed the book still unable to answer it, but infinitely more uneasy than when I started. I discovered that the human male is far more dangerous than I could ever have imagined, mainly because he does not understand just how dangerous he is. And there is no telling how much more dangerous he will become as women increasingly take over most of his natural male functions.

In this book, the term 'man' is used to refer to the human male. This seems logical. Also, much of what has been written here was made possible through the research of others. In academic texts the source of material is acknowledged by referring to the original authors in parentheses. Because this effectively breaks up any trend of thought, references have been listed, chapter by chapter, in the Bibliography.

The reader will quickly realize that the central thesis of the book is based both on speculation and evidence and I take full responsibility for this mix. I take pleasure, however, in recording an enormous debt of gratitude to all those workers whose research has made this book possible.

All those people published their results after a great deal of thought and confidence that they had done their best to ensure that what they published was as reliable as possible. In this book I am acutely aware that I have stuck my neck out with speculation. I should like to point out, however, that there are precedents, most notably the theories put forward to account for the evolution of species and for the evolution of the physical characteristics of the male and female and their functions for attracting the opposite sex. Those, like mine, were based on observation, and intended more to arouse debate than to advance an iron-clad and dogmatic view of the past, present and future of the human species.

I am also conscious of the fact that although most of our scientific and medical research is funded by public money, because of the necessary evolution of a complete (and to non-scientists abstruse) scientific language, our results are, for the most part, unavailable to the general public. Thus a vast body of fascinating knowledge remains hidden from men, women and children who have to rely on the whims of the media as to whether the results of research will be translated into a language everyone, including scientists not involved in a particular discipline, can understand. It should not be surprising, therefore, if the public purse seems to be closing; people need to know what is being done with their money, and this book is an attempt to transmit a small amount of that information. I believe scientists should think seriously about filling an enormous gap in their publishing repertoire, and widen the audience for their often intriguing and controversial data.

My own efforts could not have come this far without the support, encouragement and faith of a great many people, and I want to thank them all.

I also want to thank the very many people who talked to me about their own experiences, and who agreed to allow me to share these with you, the reader, in the hope that some good might come out of it. I cannot fully enough express my gratitude to them. In particular, I want to thank Liz Bridges, Marie Ordman, Bette Rabie and Peter Susman for reading and commenting on some of the chapters. Anne Gatti, the editor of this book, is to be congratulated on creating order out of chaos. I am grateful to David Gilmore, and to Yale University Press for permission to publish, in Chapter 2, an extract from his book *Manhood in the Making* and to T.O. Saitoti and Random House for permission to publish an extract from *The Worlds of a Masai Warrior: An Autobiography*.

Finally, I take very great pleasure in acknowledging the encouragement and patience of my sons and my wife Lorraine, who listened so patiently to some of my more outlandish theories.

1
The Coming of the Male

In February 1869, Fanny Elizabeth Potter of Kibworth near Leicester was the first woman to pass an examination as a chemist and druggist in the United Kingdom. She was the first woman in Britain officially considered competent to supervise the preparation and dispensing of medicine for human consumption. Today, in the North West Thames Regional Health Authority there are eighteen major hospitals, and in thirteen of them the principal pharmacist or contact person is a woman. Women are quietly and efficiently taking over hospital pharmacy in Great Britain and in many other countries. They should spare a moment's thought for Fanny Elizabeth Potter, on whose courage and determination in the face of Victorian male prejudice they are now capitalizing.

Let us look at other areas of the health sector. In early Victorian Britain, women doctors were unthinkable, until Elizabeth Garrett Anderson qualified in 1870, but today the average intake of female medical students approaches 50%. In Russia, women all but rule the practice of medicine. In North America the intake of female medical students has risen from 6% to 38% (in 1989). Stepping out of the health sector we can see that women are appearing in just about every sphere of hitherto male-dominated activity and are demonstrating that there is precious little the male does that they can't do as well or better. They are even turning up in the front lines when men go to war. They are tearing up the Bible in which are inscribed the commandments of male dominance.

While changing their role in society, women are constructing the still infant sociological science of Feminism. They are struggling to understand their old and new roles and are building concepts and a vocabulary to go with it. The subject is now taught in many colleges and universities. The New Feminism is the moderate outcome of the white heat of the Womens' Liberation Movement of the '60s, and the strident voices are giving way to the quieter voices of reason. Women are now turning from their introspection and gazing upon man, and are starting to ask how they are going to live together in the new world with him.

Some men, too, are worried, because at the moment men know next to nothing about themselves. It is time that the new science of gender identity embraced the study of the human male, a branch I choose to call Maleism. If justification for such a study were required, one need only have listened to the radio on 1 May, 1991 when the prestigious London cricket club, the MCC, voted to keep women out because they would spoil the 'quiet conversation of the men with their prattling'. This may stimulate amusement or frustrated annoyance, but it is a symptom of a serious problem. The question it provokes, namely why did the club members refuse to admit women, is central to the thesis of this book. I believe the answer is this: The human male is being shouldered aside, and he's fighting back. He is losing ground and he knows it. So he is hitting back, ineffectually and illogically. He is using the same weapon he has always used – violence.

Women may not know it, but they have started something big. They are taking over the human male's last hunting grounds. For the human male is and always has been a hunter. He started out hunting large animals, other men and women, and went on to hunt money, other men and women. Now women have started hunting as well, and men are going to lose their two most important prey, money and women, and they aren't allowed to hunt other men. Women are making the male redundant except as a stud and the consequences are impossible to predict. Men don't understand women and never have. They have never found it easy to cope with women when they were cooped up in the home, let alone rampant in the market place. And when the male runs into something he can't cope with, he fights.

He has already started fighting. Violent crimes against women are rising faster than at any time since the inception of records. Rape is the fastest growing crime in the United Kingdom. In Australia, reported rape cases have more than trebled in the last fifteen years. Wife abuse is endemic worldwide, and underestimated since many women refuse to report their husbands. Men are losing jobs and the violent male has grasped that the influx of women has something to do with it.

In 1989, Marc Lepine went to Montreal University and shot dead fourteen women while screaming vengeance against all womankind, and on Wednesday, 16 October, 1991, George Hennard drove his pickup truck through the front window of a restaurant in Killeen, Texas, and shot dead twenty-two people, of whom fifteen were women. Eye witnesses described how he carefully selected his victims, mainly on the basis of sex. The police later found out that he had a passionate grudge against women, calling them 'white, treacherous female vipers'. In Australia, in November 1992, a man went into a hospital with a sawn-off shotgun and killed two female members of staff.

These men weren't killing because they enjoyed it. Hennard couldn't accept the concept or consequences of his actions and committed suicide immediately afterwards. Neither he nor Lepine could know that they were responding in an extreme way to one of the most powerful biological imperatives in the human male: the need to kill.

7

Both were frustrated males; both believed their roles had been usurped by women, and both did something about it. In another age they might have vented their anger on other men or on animals. It is unlikely that either man would have attacked women had he lived in the Stone Age; in those days women did not pose a threat to the male. He was free to respond to the dictates of his maleness, and to satisfy the lust for blood which is so deeply etched into the brain of man.

If we were able to examine the brains of those two men we should probably find that they were no different from those of other men. What was different was the thinness of the veneer that, in most men, contains the biological imperative. Undeniably, man is a killer. Why else does he kill other living creatures when back home his freezer is bursting with food? Although he has evolved from primitive hunter-gatherer to a member of a sophisticated free market economy it does not necessarily follow that he has simultaneously evolved from killer to non-violent poet, artist or saint. In fact, today he still hunts, but his prey are women, money and power. He describes a good deal as a 'killing', and he 'wipes out' the opposition. He needs to use that terminology in order to satisfy the need to kill. What is disturbing is that top of his list of prey is women. The Sunday Times of 22 September, 1991 reports that the killing of women was up 24% on the previous year. According to the Director of Criminological Studies at Cardiff University, women are being 'singled out' as targets. Australian psychologist, Ronald Connay says man is reacting violently to the feeling that he is being 'bested' by women.

Given the changes in man's hunting patterns, the study of man is long overdue. We have to find out why men turn to violence, as a first step towards solving problems.

We know so much about the physiology of the female (through research done mainly by men) that we can, for example, control her sexual cycles and reproductive activity with little white pills. Yet there is no contraceptive pill for men, and one wonders just how much motivation there is to find one. This is symptomatic of man's reluctance to delve too deeply into himself.

First and foremost, man is a fertilizer of women. His need to inject his genes into a female is so strong that it dominates his life from puberty to death. This need is even stronger than the urge to kill. It is a drive that was built into him long before he became human. It could even be said that production and supply of sperm is his only *raison d'être*, and his physical power and lust to kill are directed to that end, to ensure that only the best examples of the species are propagated. If he is prevented from transmitting his genes, he becomes stressed, ill and may shut down, or go out of control. He is a most unstable, volatile and unpredictable life form, and his possession of intelligence makes him without doubt the most dangerous creature on earth.

To understand the human male we need to consider the evolutionary pressures that might have produced him, what he was originally designed for, and how he has changed (if at all) since his creation.

We can only speculate as to how the male arose as a life form. Basically, he wasn't really necessary for reproduction. For millions of years, living organisms budded off progeny which were identical in every respect to their mother. This is called asexual reproduction and it works very efficiently for relatively simple organisms such as bacteria and the amoeba. It is a particularly efficient form of reproduction because it does not require a chance meeting between a male and female, and prodigious numbers of offspring are produced. But it has disadvantages. Mutations are unlikely, since even a small change in the genetic make-up can be lethal for the species. But it also means that the species cannot adapt fast to changes in its environment and, for this reason, could become extinct.

Nevertheless, sexual reproduction happened, and became a great success. At some point in the evolution of life the necessity for a male became imperative. And all he had to do was fertilize the female to ensure the survival of the species.

From the evidence we have of ourselves and of other living creatures we can build up a scenario for the appearance of the male. The time is well over 100,000,000 years ago.

An animal, say a lizard, suns herself on a rock. Inside her body grow a number of ova or eggs. Each ovum is a single cell which contains the creature's genetic database – a complete library of information about the lizard as a species. The lizard scuttles under the rock and sits quite still. She everts an ovipositor and lays the ova or eggs. The parent moves on to eat another lizard's eggs and her own eventually hatch into progeny all identical to the parent. This is parthenogenesis, or asexual reproduction. All these genotypes have evolved over millions of years in a tough, hostile environment and they produce creatures which are well adapted to survive. Their genotype is proven stuff. Because no hybrids are formed there is less chance of introducing a potentially lethal gene or mutation of an existing one.

But it is a tough world. Vast herds of voracious egg-eating predators sweep the land or sea, gobbling up eggs as fast as they can be laid. The wind may uncover them, expose them to an unbelievably hot sun and the predators have to eat them hard-boiled. Species are becoming extinct at a tremendous rate. Some, however, have evolved tricks to keep the egg-eaters out.

Consider, for example, the hypothetical viviparous virgin lizard or VVL. The VVL has survived because she does not lay her eggs but keeps them inside her body where they are warm, wet and safe unless the VVL herself is snapped up by a passing predator. The eggs hatch out in the VVL's body and she keeps them until they are old enough to look after themselves. When the time comes she extrudes a long exit tube through which the little VVLs pass, and when they are outside they scatter.

But, as mentioned before, it is a very hard life and one must adapt or die out. It's one thing to produce a clutch of immature eggs, lay them and go on your way rejoicing; quite another to play host to a battery of developing lizards all living off you. They swell you up, slow you down and before you can shed the load you're a free lunch.

One strain of VVL, however, has developed a neat trick. One VVL will allow another VVL to insert her ovipositor into her own and lay her eggs inside her. This has tremendous possibilities. The lizard who has thus off-loaded her eggs into the comparative safety of another lizard's body is free to concentrate on other things. This, however, is not satisfactory for the recipient who has to carry the eggs. Fortunately, the act of inserting the ovipositor is fun and instead of moving on, the egg depositor stays around to feed the recipient VVL which has to spend some time under a rock until the baby VVLs make their appearance. Then they can have some more fun. This, however, is not sexual reproduction. But it's a start.

Inside the reproductive tract of the recipient VVL some evolutionary changes are taking place. The donor's ova and the recipient's are in close proximity. Each contains the full set of chromosomes. Some of the ova fuse to form hybrids. Most of these do not survive to hatch. But others do. Some ova contain only half the genetic material required to produce another VVL and normally they would not survive. But when two incomplete ova, one from each VVL, fuse, an egg is formed which contains the full chromosomal complement. The egg hatches and a live

VVL emerges with characteristics of both donor and recipient. This is the birth of sexual reproduction. Ova from donor and recipient are henceforth referred to as gametes. The donor's gamete is the sperm and the recipient's gamete is an oocyte. They have been formed by a process called meiosis, whereby a cell divides into parts, each of which contains half the genetic database. This is a new ball game and compared with asexual reproduction it is complex and very chancy.

The idea that ova might have fused inside the recipient's reproductive tract is interesting. But it begs some important questions. For example, why didn't ova from the same VVL fuse? How did they get close enough to fuse? And how were some formed with only half the full genomic set? These are tough questions to which we have, as yet, no answers. But why not keep the hypothesis flying a little longer and see where it leads?

In order for sexual reproduction to succeed, the two gametes would have to meet reliably. The answer may be in size and number. It is possible that each VVL produced gametes i.e. ova in a whole range of sizes. Size would be important. The larger gametes had the better chance of surviving. If two small gametes fused, the fertilized egg died through a lack of nutrients. Thus larger gametes contained more food to keep them alive. But the larger the gamete the more sluggish it was. Think of what would happen if men ejaculated a few large, slow-moving pellets instead of feverish little spermatozoa. Apart from the discomfort, the chances of the pellet making it up the vagina and into the fallopian tubes to an equally slow-moving ovum would be small and the species wouldn't have a chance. Thus it is possible that the most successful fusions involved those between a small, agile gamete from one VVL and a larger gamete from another. But a small gamete has a statistically smaller chance of bumping into a large one in a dark, wide tunnel. And so, the VVL which produced lots of fast little gametes was selected over time, and during mating she transmitted these *en masse* to another VVL which specialized in fewer, larger gametes. This is in fact what happens now. The male sperm are relatively small, very agile and are produced in hundreds of millions. The ovum is much larger than the spermatozoon, travels slowly and only one is usually released each month by the human female.

The whole business sounds so complicated compared with asexual reproduction that no self-respecting bookmaker would give odds on its evolving. Yet sexual reproduction took off in style. Why?

There are some advantages. For one thing, sexual populations will evolve faster than asexual ones. If a favourable mutant pops up in an individual, say a gene which will boost intelligence, it has a greater chance of spreading in a sexual population through recombination. We all know of the calculating fictional character, usually a woman, who consciously decides to choose the most intelligent man she can find to father her child. She knows what she's doing. She's being driven by powerful evolutionary forces.

A population that reproduces sexually will also be at an advantage in resisting evolutionary changes. Most mutations in the genes are potentially dangerous. They could alter, in a deleterious fashion, the fitness of the individual to survive. The holes in the ozone layer allow dangerous levels of ionizing radiation to reach us and these might cause totally unforeseen mutations. Certain chemicals, for example benzene, can cause unpredictable changes. In an asexual population where the genotype is transmitted faithfully, unaltered from generation to generation, the members are stuck with the mutation which could wipe out the species altogether. In sexual reproduction, however, the dangerous gene is diluted through recombination and edited out of the genotype. It is not surprising, therefore, that all mammals use only sexual reproduction.

In keeping the eggs inside her body the VVL was making a major economic commitment. She was prepared to siphon off a lot of her own energy and minerals to nurture her young, and it limited her.

No man complains that he needs a break from his spermatogenesis. Making gametes, be they sperm or oocytes is not a big drain on the system. But sheltering and feeding a growing baby inside your own body is another matter. The pregnant VVL was no longer as mobile; she may have found it difficult to hunt and protect herself. She needed help.

Enter the male.

The female who made tiny, energetic gametes which she shot in great numbers into other females never got pregnant. Her turnover of gametes was high and within days, perhaps hours of copulation, she was hunting for another female. She was the forerunner, the proto-male.

During this process behaviour too was being selected. Role-splitting made new demands and if these could not be met the species would be doomed. The proto-male who tended to protect his female and her young from predators was selected, and of these the strongest and fiercest was preferred. Gradually the male found his role. He was a modified female and so he retained much of her form and function. He looked basically like a female. But some important changes were taking place. He did a lot of fighting. He had to fight off predators, some much larger than he was. He was constantly being challenged by other males. Females weren't all that thick on the ground. They tended to shelter in holes, under rocks or in trees, depending on the species. His muscles had to be harder and bigger. He became heavier, longer, or taller than the female. He had to swim long distances, run many miles, see further over the long grass to find food and females. He became a hunter.

14

His sexual habits became different from those of the female. He covered a lot of territory and encountered many females. Nature had already seen to it that the rewards of copulation included a wonderful orgasm and he became promiscuous. He spread his genes indiscriminately and the species spread. Neither did he limit his sexual practices to members of his own species. He used his strength to force his attentions on whatever attracted him, male or female. If he was a male worth his salt he coupled with anything that moved him. But these matings were sterile. Even today echoes of the indiscriminate proto-male reverberate in the mind of the male. Why else should a man have been arrested in England in 1991 for swimming up to a dolphin called Freddie, masturbating it and rubbing his groin up against its erect penis?

Through his aggressive nature the male VVL limited his lifespan. The female outlived him. Not all males fought, however. Those who shied away from fights for females and hid away from predators would outlive their braver fellows. But they would not copulate and their genes would die out with them.

So much for the VVL and a hypothetical account of how the male of the species happened. Essentially the male is a modified female. Eve's rib, not Adam's. The hypothesis is not, however, snatched from thin air but is drawn from the study of modern man and from male behaviour in other animals. Take, for example, the insertion of a tube into another creature for purposes other than insemination. There are creatures which still do it. The female sea horse drops her eggs into a pouch carried by the male. And leaping straight to man himself: if statistics could be taken, they might reveal that men have sex more for pleasure than for making babies. They insert their penis into women because they enjoy it so much. Clearly women enjoy it too, otherwise they wouldn't let men do it just for fun. This behaviour may have nothing to do with procreation.

The promiscuity of the proto-man has been transmitted faithfully down through millions of years directly to modern man. The ancestral drive to roam in search of sex is as powerful in man as it was in the proto-male. He is constantly looking for sex with single-minded intensity. He will sweep aside all other considerations. Why else would men who have attained the pinnacle of success in their careers, men whose veneer of civilization would seem to be impenetrable, men with beautiful wives and caring families, take to the streets in search of copulation with a prostitute? The answer, simply, is that they are on a genetic leash, pulled by the dictates of their primitive maleness. They are doing what comes naturally to the human male. And if we examine virtually all males, from the hangingfly to the human, as shall be done in succeeding chapters, we shall recognize the proto-male over and over again. He is the hunter, the seeker of sex. And in order to help him find her, the female had to change as well.

In creating the male, the female had introduced tremendous problems for herself. No longer was she independent. The female needed to attract the male. Going out to find him was dangerous because of predators and she was no fighter. It was safer to wait for him to find her. She couldn't bellow in the hope that he'd hear her. The chances were that she'd get all the predators in the neighbourhood salivating. Neither could she don bright colours for the same reason. She had to use something quiet that only the male of her species would recognize. The answer was perfume. The female of many species releases a mixture of powerful volatile hormones called pheromones which are carried on the breeze to the sensors of the male who recognizes them instantly and homes in on the transmitter. This voyage, of course, puts the male at risk and many a moth has been snapped up while winging to his love.

Once the female had attracted the male, she had other problems. There was always the chance that the male she'd attracted was being followed by a predator who would make a meal out of them both.

She might attract several males who could all arrive at the same time. Anyone who has seen three or four drakes simultaneously trying to penetrate a duck while fighting furiously over her body will know the problem. Furthermore, she might draw a runt. Undersized weakling males lust as passionately as he-men and can be a nuisance to a female who is shopping for quality in genes.

To the male this was just another sperm spray. Any female would do for a one-night stand. But it was a different matter for the female. She was going to invest a lot in this mating. If she mated with a poor specimen she might produce weak or dead offspring. During her period of gestation she would be out of action and if a better guy turned up the following day she wouldn't be able to take advantage of his presence. Therefore the female selected only the brightest, biggest, noisiest and toughest males that came her way. This created problems for the males.

Large males with bright colours and the best songs don't live long. The flashy male also attracts predators, so life is fun but short for him. The male peacock who spreads his spectacular tail feathers and pulls in the birds also shows a passing eagle the way to lunch. The small male zebra finch who dazzles the female with an outpouring of song also impresses a predator which gets two for the price of one. The female zebra finch, incidentally, does not sing. Consider also the long-tailed widowbird that adorns the grasslands of Kenya. If the tail feathers are cut off the males and glued on to the tails of other male widowbirds, the females will prefer to nest in the territories of males with the abnormally long tails. Clearly the longer the tail, the more the female likes it. This, of course, attracts predators. In evolutionary terms, therefore, an intermediate-sized tail will have been selected, the balance being provided by the female and the predator.

The female's problems did not end with the termination of foreplay. There was added danger for both sexes in the act of mating, especially if they were little. The male learned to copulate fast. When you're small and on top of a female you're fair game for passing predators. The rat mounts, penetrates and ejaculates within seconds. The bank vole scurries along concealed runs on the floor of the forest and barely breaks off his trip to fertilize a passing female. Birds flit together and break off so fast that it seems inconceivable that the male could have found his way through all those feathers. Larger animals can afford to be more leisurely. The lion knows he is not going to need to look over his shoulder, and takes his time, as does the elephant and the rhinoceros.

But more serious was the fact that in creating the male the female had introduced complications into her life completely unrelated to the act of sex or its biological consequences. These problems, which will be dealt with in more detail in later chapters, can be summarised as follows:

1. The male had ideas of his own – he didn't take no for an answer.
2. The male became possessive. He wanted to collect females who were herded together and sequestered for the benefit of one male.
3. In some cases the male took over the role of the female who was used simply as a sex object and driven away after the mating.
4. Sexual reproduction involves a transaction between two individuals. Therefore it is potentially corrupting and it wasn't long after the introduction of sex that the female discovered the male wanted it so badly he was prepared to pay for it.

5. Conceivably the most serious complication for the human female was that she fell in love. She completely lost control over her own very impressive creation.

And when the first human male stepped out into the sun he *was* impressive. He was tough, handsome, brave and intelligent. He was ruthless, lusty and murderous and the world was his oyster. He could outthink and outmanoeuvre any other creature on earth and he revelled in hunting and killing them. He was thus supremely well equipped to perform his primary purpose, which was to fertilize and protect the female and his progeny until the latter could take care of themselves. He did this without asking himself why, and he did it driven by an emotion which he did not understand, but which ruled his mind and which was more important to him than anything else. It is an emotion that we call pride, and pride made him exult in the awareness of his success. Without pride he could never have succeeded.

He grew up in a group. Men were smart enough to realize that survival depended on the group and not on the individual, and so they suppressed the urge to kill each other and herded their women and children together in small communities. Life was tough and absolute obedience from women and children was demanded. Women yielded, being totally dependent on men for their survival. A pattern was established. The men hunted large, dangerous animals in groups and food was shared. But not the women. Each man had his own woman whom he guarded fiercely and with whom he and he alone copulated. This was a most powerful drive, an imperative laid down millions of years before in the proto-male fanatical about guarding his genes.

But it was different on safari. If a male happened upon a lone woman she was fair game, since he had no regard for another man's genes, especially if that man was unknown to him and not around at the time. If the woman fancied him a mutually satisfactory union could be effected within half an hour. If she didn't he'd take her anyway. Since men hunted in groups, a woman rash enough to go for a long walk stood a reasonable chance of being gang raped.

The male grew up and learned by example. He was brought up mainly by women, who clothed and fed him, and taught him his language. Men fashioned toy weapons for him which girls were forbidden to play with, a rule enforced by women. Girls learned how to make clothes and prepare food. Women directed the male's play to manly things and strongly discouraged any sign of preference for girls' games.

When he was old enough, he was initiated into the hunt. His hormones flared up and he fought with other boys for the girl he fancied.

The women were kept tightly in rein but they were held in awe for their powers of reproduction. The female form became the symbol of plenty, and the gods men first worshipped were female. Unfortunately there was a high turnover in women. The death rate in childbirth was high, and the shortage could and did become a matter of grave concern. Consequently raids were carried out on other communities. Bitter fights were fought and women carried off to make good the deficit. Women were not asked if they wanted to go. They had to adapt to their new home and men. This was the crucible in which the role of women was formed.

It probably wasn't always cosy in the cave. In some communities a single male might lord it over a group of females, including his own daughters, whom he would copulate with and terrorize. He would be large, strong and fiercely indepedent. He might even kill his male offspring to prevent them from learning from his example and killing him to take over the harem.

But on the whole, the lot of women under cave-dwelling man was comparatively good. He stuck to one woman, respected her and made no undue physical demands. Her workload was comparatively light and her greatest dangers were from death in childbirth, disease and raids by men from other groups. But all that changed when someone in the Middle East discovered how to make bread.

Suddenly people could eat grass. All they had to do was find a field of it, thresh out the seeds, pulverize them to flour, mix it with water and eat it. Better still, the goo could be moulded into lumps and baked on a hot stone to make a portable foodstuff that managed to keep people alive. Then some bright spark noticed that where seeds fell more grass grew. But it became even better. If grass could be grown for people it could also be grown, and stored, for animals, especially the tasty ones with wool. This was the birth of farming, and it sealed the fate of women for the next 10,000 years.

No longer was it necessary to live a nomadic life, to follow the game and die of starvation if the group couldn't keep up. Provided they had a bag of seeds and a river nearby, they could hang up their hats and set up home. Irrigation heralded civilization.

But life was still dangerous. If anything it became more so, the greatest threat being posed by roaming bands of people looking for a home. So men still needed their weapons to protect their farms and their families, and they formed small vigilante groups which were the forerunners of the vast armies that were to sweep the Middle East and Asia. Also, men found farming pretty boring after the thrill of the hunt. They needed a handy, cheap and manageable source of labour. They didn't have to look far.

Women were set to work in the fields as soon as they were old enough to do so. Men ploughed the land, and even for this job they used another animal, the ox, to do the hard work of pulling the plough, which they simply guided through the line of earth. After that, the women sowed, watered, harvested and threshed. They pounded the grain, and do so to this day in primitive farming communities. They stored the flour and baked the bread.

Men prospered. They produced more than they consumed, generated wealth and cultivated more land. They introduced currency and trade, and business was born. It was only men who traded and fixed prices. It didn't even occur to them that women could take part in this process. Women had far too much to do at home.

Wealth created undreamed of possibilities for men. Provided they could afford to keep them, they could have as many women as they wanted. The more land a man had, the more women he needed to work it. He bought these women from poorer families who could not afford to keep their women. Boys were no problem, since they were recruited into the many private armies needed to protect a man's property, or for raiding purposes.

A woman bought was a woman owned, body and soul. It was inconceivable that she should refuse her owner's carnal demands. She had to honour and obey. But she was a commodity with a difference.

Women were not just a pool of labour. They were a source of physical pleasure, and their children proclaimed their owner's virility, a property of the male that he valued above virtually all else, and one that could be appreciated by other men.

At last men had everything, the rich ones anyway. They could reproduce their own genes, protect their women and their young, and be promiscuous into the bargain. No wonder men wanted to be rich.

A woman had no choice but to make the best of it. She could think as well as any man and she knew it. But she also knew that he was physically more than a match for her. So she made the most of what she had. She made her home her university and she majored in the male. She learned how to refine the art of playing on a man's pride. She encouraged his vanities, and built up his confidence, aware that his failure meant her downfall. She praised his strength and virility, even if she had to sleep surreptitiously with another man to produce an issue for her impotent master. She guided him into delegating to her the running of the home and convinced him (no difficult task) that she was more suited to it than he was. In a home of many women, the most intelligent and ruthless woman dominated.

In time different societies evolved, but a universal pattern seems to have been established. The male was taught by women to believe they are born to be housekeepers, nurses and cooks. And life went on much the same for thousands of years until men started doing things that were so interesting that women wanted to do them as well. Women watched men having fun with medicine, science, literature and the arts and cursed the monotony of their lives. But when they expressed an interest in joining in, they were shocked by the violence with which they were excluded. Perhaps they didn't realise that men were still hunters who no longer had animals to hunt, and instead made knowledge, wealth (and women) their prey. When the lust for blood could not be denied men went to war, but during periods of peace they needed to keep busy with manly things, and women were not invited. Anyway, everyone knew that women weren't able to think like men. Hadn't women told men that often enough?

2
A God on Earth

A true story: Julia lived with her husband Sebastian in a large house in Hampstead in London. Their children had grown up and moved away. Julia had just gone through a bad menopause and had been advised by her doctor not to take hormone replacement therapy due to an increased risk of cancer in her case. To take her mind off her physical problems, Julia threw herself into the task of decorating the house which they had just moved into, and Sebastian encouraged her with a virtually unlimited budget. When she had done the job and the house looked superb, Sebastian informed her that he was leaving her for his secretary. He told her he wanted more children and needed a younger woman. He bought her a small house in Kilburn, a much poorer suburb, settled £1000 a month on her and told her that was all she was getting. One week after he had completed the sale on the small house in Kilburn, he had a taxi waiting for her outside his house. Julia moved into her new home without a murmur and slid into a nervous breakdown.

In other chapters I explore the forces that may have created men like Sebastian, the changes in their bodies as they develop, their effects on women, and, more importantly today, the effects on men of the emerging freedom of women. In this chapter I ask what is important to man, what his soul may be made of, the nature of the creature called Sebastian. I believe this is most important in trying to understand how he established and maintained his supremacy over women. It will also help us to understand how dangerous man will become as he loses his means of expressing his maleness while retaining the inner gods that drive him to prove to himself and to other men that he is a man.

The adult human male is the most powerful creature on earth. He has achieved supreme dominance through a combination of physical strength, selfishness and intelligence, which enabled him to fashion the tools and make the plans which put him where he is today. From the time he first appeared to the present day man has run the longest and most tyrannical dictatorship the world has ever experienced. It has lasted over 100,000 years. There is no evidence that men anywhere allowed themselves consistently to be ruled by women, or that women ever made any decisions which materially altered the course of civilization. Human society has in the main been designed, modified and run by the male. He has seldom if ever turned to women for advice or help with matters outside the domestic sphere. Indeed, he laid down the limits of their involvement in all activity outside the home and family.

All the major discoveries that dictated the progress of humanity were probably made by men, for the simple reason that they did not allow any input from women. Credit for key inventions such as the wheel and the production of fire cannot be taken by either sex, but are implicitly assumed to be the product of man's ingenuity. Even if they had been discovered by women, it is unlikely that contemporary males would have acknowledged their contribution. The first wheel was probably a slice from a tree trunk, cut by men. Men who chipped flint for weapons, which women were not allowed to make, started fires by accident and so discovered how to make fires at will. In most primitive societies that have been studied, women traditionally do not make weapons, mine or quarry, carve or paint for ornamental purposes or manufacture musical instruments. On the other hand, in these societies the jobs of grain grinding, water carrying, herb and seed gathering, cooking and food preservation, weaving and pottery manufacture are done almost exclusively by women.

Women were barred from the councils of men; in few Amerind societies was a woman admitted to a pow wow except under extraordinary circumstances. Similarly, in Africa, South America, the Middle and Far East, there is no evidence that women played a significant role in decision-taking at any level.

There have been some exceptions, but if anything they prove the rule. Such a worldwide distribution of male-oriented power is remarkable and cannot be explained by the migration of an idea. It is, rather, the inevitable result of a power imbalance in favour of man.

At a more personal level, men exercise seemingly absolute power over the lives of women. When most women link their lives with those of men, they surrender their personal freedom virtually completely. Men often decide where their women will live, how many children they will have, how much money they will spend, and even what clothes they will wear. Women who live with men are usually so dependent on them that they dare not leave their men for fear of compromising their own survival. Consequently they will suffer ill treatment, to the point of crippling violence, in silence, and will refuse to testify against their husbands even when their mouths are so damaged that they can hardly frame their words.

What gave man the edge? How was he able to establish and maintain for so long an absolute supremacy over women? The answer is not to be found in arguments about power structures, politics or sociologically based theories but in the human body. It is a matter of physiology, more precisely of biochemistry. The plight of women can be ascribed to a single chemical, the male sex hormone testosterone. This one hormone, created by the female and placed in the body of the male, sealed her fate for millions of years thereafter. It is the hormone that turns a boy into a man, that gives his muscles bulk and strength, stokes his aggression and drives his search for sexual gratification. Testosterone stimulates the growth spurt that makes a man taller than a woman, it causes the male sex organs to enlarge, it deepens the voice, stimulates the production of red blood cells and creates the typically male pattern of body hair. Testosterone, through its anabolic effects, may be what causes the male brain to grow larger than that of the female.

Women, too, have testosterone in the circulation, but nowhere near enough to give them the male physical characteristics. What testosterone is to the male, oestradiol, the female sex hormone, is to the woman. This hormone causes all the changes that turn a girl into an adult woman. As well as stimulating the growth of the internal reproductive organs and the breasts, oestradiol promotes the pubertal growth of the labia majora and labia minora. It causes breast enlargement and linear bone growth, but because the ends or epiphyses of the bones are more sensitive to oestradiol than they are to testosterone, they close sooner in women, which explains why women are usually smaller than men. Oestradiol enlarges the hips and widens the pelvic inlet, which facilitates birth. It also lays down fat – women have twice the fat mass that men do, while having only two-thirds the muscle and bone mass of men.

And yet if we were to look at the chemical structures of testosterone and oestradiol the differences are negligible. The two hormones are almost identical in structure, differing only in terms of a single carbon atom and a handful of hydrogen atoms.

It is easy to conceive how the VVL of Chapter 1 could have designed testosterone from her own oestradiol. And yet those apparently insignificant differences in structure enslaved women, and may continue to do so for another 10,000 years or more.

Boys and girls are born at about the same weight. A survey in England and Wales gave the average weight of boys at birth as 3.42 kg (7.53 lb), and girls as 3.28 kg (7.21 lb). Boys attain their maximum height between 18 and 19 years, and girls between 14 and 18 years. Male physical power peaks at about 20 years of age, and then falls off. By the age of 29, a man has lost about 25% of his muscle mass. In men and women of 20 years, body fat is about 30% of total weight; in men this stays constant, while in women the proportion of fat will rise to about 50% by the time they reach 50. In Britain, a 20-year-old man of 5 ft 9 in. is likely to weigh around 69 kg (153 lb), while a woman of similar age and height will weigh about 63 kg (140 lb), the difference reflecting muscle mass.

Girls are said to mature intellectually at an earlier age than boys. They are ready to bear children in their early to mid-teens, and in many primitive and developing countries young girls of 12 and upwards may be sold or given to men as brides.

Throughout their period of reproductive activity, women are at the mercy of their sex. During prehistoric and later centuries, many women were pregnant for most of the months of their child-bearing years. Due to poor nutrition and lack of knowledge they were undernourished and ill, since the foetus drew from their bodies the food it needed and depleted them. Many pregnant women died through disease, malnutrition or miscarriage, and, if they survived the gestational period, often died in childbirth. Consequently the women of the past had their hands full without having time to sit back and wonder about their role in the cave, hut, hovel, long hut or castle.

Once the baby was born they had to suckle it, look after it and clean up the mess it made. There just wasn't time to think about power-sharing, let alone do anything about it. And apart from child-minding, the women were required to make thread and clothing with the skins, needles and knives the men had made for them. With the advent of farming women were still required to carry out these functions, and in addition they had to make bread with the corn, wheat or rye that the men dumped outside the home. Any woman who rebelled was thrashed into submission by her stronger husband or carried back to her parents with a demand for a refund for defective goods.

Women have a limited reproductive lifespan, and become sterile after menopause, when their ovaries cease to produce oestradiol and ova. This 'change of life' is accompanied by mood changes, drying and wrinkling of the skin, atrophy of the sex organs, drying of the vagina and osteoporosis, all caused by the loss of oestradiol. After a session of irregular appearances, their periods cease. When this happens, their attractiveness to the male who wants to propagate his genes may cease or lessen considerably, and in many cultures he takes a younger wife while retaining, if he can, the older woman for her administrative abilities in the home. It is not unknown for men in western cultures to engineer a split between themselves and their ageing wives in order to find a younger, more attractive and fertile woman.

But things are changing. Today women can counteract the effects of the menopause by taking hormone replacement therapy (HRT) in the form of small doses of oestrogens and progesterone, and thus retain some of their youthful form and appearance. But even HRT may not satisfy the male who lusts after a younger woman.

Women can now decide when to become pregnant due to the discovery by men of the oral contraceptives (OCs). At a stroke, men have handed women their liberation from thousands of years of reproductive bondage. Women can choose when to become pregnant, if at all. Their bodies have been liberated from reproductive toil and they can direct their energies to other things. Quite conceivably, the Women's Movement owes its success in large measure to the OC. Just as the use of lead plumbing might have contributed to the downfall of the Roman Empire, so may the little white tablets that women swallow every night topple man from his throne.

Man's position as dominant figure in the household has much to do with his superior physical strength. Man has revelled in his muscles ever since he discovered what they could do. His first unit of measurement was the unit of strength. The man who lifted the heavy stone above his shoulders was the leader, the chief, the king. No woman could get the stone off the ground, let alone above her knees. In any event, no woman was permitted to touch the sacred stone. It was part of a bigger thing: the search by man for the meaning of what it is to be a man.

This question seems to have been resolved by most male members of communities both ancient and modern as a trial of strength. Men are not recognized by other men or by women to have attained manhood unless they have attempted to attain a culturally imposed ideal. In order to lay claim to his prize of manhood, to cross the threshold that separates the boy from the man, the boy must pit himself against danger, pain, the fear of death, or of ridicule and contempt; he will have to show that he can and will use his muscles. There is no parallel for this behaviour in the world of women. They are not expected to demonstrate their worthiness except as incubators for babies. They might also measure up to standards of perceived morality, but they will never be asked to prove their womanhood through the brave and intelligent use of arms, legs and hands.

The rituals that men have designed in order to turn their boys into men provide a window into the rooms in their minds where they store their key ideas about the nature of manhood. It is worth examining some examples of the rites of passage to which boys are subjected in order to turn them into men. These rituals underlie the concept of a change in identity, a form of rebirth, as it was called by a pioneer of manhood studies, Arnold von Gennep, in his book *The Rites of Passage*. He interpreted these rites as a form of death of the boy and a rebirth as a man. He saw them in three stages: separation from women and from childhood, change, and establishment of the man. The boy must reject his maternal input, renounce his mother and be taken away from her by force, if need be. Next he is placed in a kind of no-man's-land where he is neither man nor boy, where his body will be prepared by ordeal for the entry of the man. Finally, he leaves his place of isolation and can practise as a man.

A Masai boy on the plains of Africa that lie on the borders of Tanzania and Kenya was not a man until he had killed a lion with his spear. He was not allowed to go into battle until he had dipped his spearpoint into the blood of his own lion. Indeed, some boys would not be allowed to enter the initiation ceremonies and ordeals until they had killed a dangerous animal.

The Masai do not believe that manhood is inevitable. It has to be deliberately induced. A door has to be opened which they call the 'door to manhood'. During the period of their testing, the boys are called the *moran*. They have to be fiercest in defending their village against attack by other men or by predators such as rhino, elephant and lions. They will also have to endure circumcision without flinching. The ceremony is graphically described by a Masai man, Tepilit Ole Saitoti, who is told: 'Do not budge. Do not move a muscle or even blink. You can face only one direction until the operation is completed. The slightest movement on your part will mean that you are a coward, incompetent and unworthy to be a Masai man.' Significantly, although Masai girls are also circumcised, they are not required to show such fortitude and restraint. If they do cry out, they will not be stigmatized. It is not uncommon for men to have to hold down the struggling and kicking girls.

The *moran* might also wish to demonstrate his sexual prowess. Saitoti describes how a young *moran* tried out his newly discovered sexuality on an older woman:

'He put a bold move on her. At first the woman could not believe his intention, or rather was amazed by his courage. The name of the warrior was Ngengeiya, or Drizzle.

"Drizzle, what do you want?"

"To make love to you."

"I am your mother's age."

"It's either her or you."

This remark took the woman by surprise. She had underestimated the saying, "there is no such thing as a young warrior." When you are a warrior, you are expected to perform bravely in any situation. Your age and size are immaterial.

"You mean you could really love me like a grown-up man?"

"Try me woman."

He moved in on her. Soon the woman started moaning with excitement, calling his name. "Honey Drizzle, Honey Drizzle, you are a man." In a breathy, stammering voice, she said, "A real man."'

In Ethiopia, the Amhara tribe call masculinity *wand-nat*. This quality of *wand-nat* is demonstrated by teenage boys in a ceremony called *buhe* in which they whip each other until the blood flows. The rest of the tribe look on, and any boy who cries out or cowers is jeered and his reputation as a man destroyed. The boys prove their indifference to pain by burning hot embers into their limbs. Whipping of boys as a test of manhood is also practised by the Pueblo Indians of New Mexico, an otherwise peaceful people.

Young men of the Sioux tribe threaded the skin with thongs and, if they went deeper, the pectoral muscles of the chest. Then they tied these to a post and stepped backwards until they had ripped themselves free.

In Namibia, formerly called South West Africa, the boys of the pygmy !Kung Bushmen are not allowed to take a bride until they have found and killed an antelope single-handed. In addition, they are taken away from their mothers in order to make them reborn as men. This idea of being reborn is very common among many tribes. It requires the removal of a boy from the influence of the mother, the deleting of the feminine in the boy in order that the man can enter his body. The !Kung send their boys into the bush where they must survive or die. Clearly this has practical value in a community which relies for its survival on the ability of its men to hunt. But there is, in addition, the mystical component, the swapping of the soul of the boy for that of the man. The boy is made to endure extremes of temperature, hunger and thirst. He is made to dance continuously to the point of exhaustion. The period of initiation lasts six weeks. During this time he must not see his mother or get any help from his father. Interestingly, he must also learn about his environment; he must assimilate the names of the plants and animals about him, in order that he may survive.

This quest for intellectual attainment is very unusual as a rite of passage for boys, and has a parallel among the Jews, who place much emphasis on mental rather than physical skills as a means of producing a man. The Jewish boy is put on trial, usually at the age of thirteen. He is required to show not physical endurance or strength, but the qualities of mental stamina, alertness and intellectual ability which will be needed in order to survive as a man. Although the Jews have shown themselves since biblical times to be fierce, intelligent and dreaded warriors if the need arose, the emphasis in Jewish communities, no matter

34

where they have been established, has been on intellectual and academic attainment, and the use of intelligence in commerce. The highest status is accorded to the learned scholar, the professor, the doctor, the successful business-man. Less tribute is paid to the warrior or the sportsman.

The reverse is true in those societies where war or raiding is deeply rooted in the culture. Here an extraordinary premium is put on the concept of masculi-nity. Consider, for example, the Sambia people who live as hunters and gardeners on the steep slopes of the mountainous regions of what is now Papua New Guinea. In the dense, luxuriant forests the men, but not the women, are allowed to hunt the small mammals which form part of their diet. Formerly fierce and probably cannibalistic hunters, they are forbidden by law to raid and kill their neighbours, and are forced to relive the warrior skills of their ancestors vicariously in the form of legend and folklore. They are a primitive tribal community who are exceptionally preoccupied with the qualities that make a man, and with the rites of passage that transform a boy into a man. Their men do not regard manhood as a natural development but as a state of being imposed through ritual. Without the ritual, the boy remains a boy all his life.

The Sambian men subject their boys to ordeals of strength and pain, but in addition they force the boys to commit the act of fellatio, in order to drink the ejaculate from old men that will enable them to grow and become strong. If they do not drink the semen they will remain puny and weak. The men do not do this as a homosexual practice from which to derive pleasure, but purely as a means of injecting manhood into the boys. The boys also have to endure quite horrendous rituals of pain, in which reeds are pushed up their nostrils until the blood flows. Boys must demonstrate their indifference to injury, in preparation for the day when they will fight as warriors.

Clearly, in a primitive hunting or farming society the

rites of passage are part of the strategies for survival in a hostile environment. Boys are taught how to take their place as providers and protectors of the community. The need for this is recognized by all, including the women. But equally, a lot of unnecessary suffering is inflicted, and a great deal of mystique surrounds the voyage from boy to manhood. Men fear the debilitating influence of the woman. They worry that if the boy stays with his mother the boy will never die and the man will never enter his body. He will stay weak and useless and will need to be supported as though he too were a woman.

There are striking similarities in the form of the ritual in male rites of passage whether they are practised in Africa or thousands of miles away in New Guinea. It appears that the principles behind these rituals are deeply ingrained in men's minds, and it leads one to ask how men will react if the rites of passage no longer relate to the life of the tribe, due to their increased contact with a rapidly changing world.

Presumably, if, as has happened in Africa and New Guinea, the men are forbidden to carry out their manly practices of killing other men and hunting wild animals, the form of the ritual may change. It is unlikely that the ritual will be dropped. The values, if not the methods, will be retained. The initiation may gradually fall away as a formalised ceremony, but the need to have one will always be there. Men will find other rituals, and if they are anything like those they have practised in the past, they will be punishing for the boy, and their effects may not be as limited as they have been in the past. Also, the men may become less inclined to direct these initiations, and the boys will formulate and enact their own rites. We may be seeing this in our western societies.

In western cultures, apart from the ritual circumcision and Bar Mitzvah of the Jewish people, there are very few if any formal and clearly overt counterparts to the primitive ceremonies of the Masai and the Amhara. But they are there nevertheless, and they are run by the boys themselves. Boys play games, but they are very serious games, in which they pit themselves against other boys, men or against risk of death or injury. In Britain boys steal cars and joyride while their friends look on approvingly. When I was a boy we played the game of chicken, in which we drove motor cycles at each other at speeds of up to 80 miles per hour, and the first to swerve was a chicken. At sixteen years we sat in a circle and drew razor blades across our fingers and palms. No boy who was prepared to sit at the circle flinched from drawing blood. Some boys boasted about their exploits with girls or women, but since they could not prove these with a bloodstained bridal sheet they were usually not believed. Boys who watched films such as *Rebel Without a Cause* with James Dean, borrowed their father's cars and played chicken. In the film *Saturday Night Fever*, a boy who is desperate to prove his manhood falls to his death during a tightrope display on a New York bridge.

In all Western cultures boys play these ritual games. Something draws them to the rite of passage. Is it a genetic heritage, the manifestation of the action of testosterone on a male-imprinted brain? Would girls do it if they were dosed up with testosterone? We don't know. We don't know why we played those games. Perhaps we were putting ourselves through a trial of strength to prepare ourselves for the struggle to survive in the world of business. Significantly, our games were unsupervised by men who may have tried to stop them. Yet these same men probably sat in their own circles, told their own tales, risked death and mutilated themselves, driven by the same primitive drumbeat as are their sons. Some Englishmen do put their sons through an informal test of manhood – those who take their sons to the pub to show them how to down a pint. Perhaps some of these fathers also covertly approve of their sons' joyriding exploits. Perhaps they subconsciously miss the opportunity to initiate their sons into manhood. It is a curious turnabout: in contrast to the close, tightly-knit and obsessive preoccupation of primitive man with his son, modern western man abandons this aspect of his son's education, if it can be called that.

With one possible exception. Man may be teaching his sons by example, ritual by proxy. Anthony Burgess's book *A Clockwork Orange* showed the way. Teenagers break into a woman's apartment and rape her in style. The rape is a ritual. The boys are going through their rite of passage. And this is one which modern man can prepare his sons for by doing it himself. He has very few options left. He cannot hunt animals for there are none. He cannot raid another village and return home triumphantly with his spoils. Bank robbery is a poor substitute. But he can show his manhood by raping a woman. Men who rape are notching up a kill on the butt of the gun, doing something that they can prepare their sons for. They do it unconsciously; no rapist regards himself as a shaman. But, is he not creating another yardstick, another unit of measurement for the modern boy? In a world in which all the units of strength are becoming obsolete, and in which those that remain are drifting out of reach through competition by women, surely the one which still remains attainable is the rape index.

This may seem an abhorrent idea to Hampstead or San Fransisco Man, even to Sebastian, but there are other men in the world who are closer to the primitive male, or more honest with him. Boys will seize upon the rape index; they already have. Teenage rape is not unknown, especially as a group activity. It may even be argued that gang rape is a form of manhood ritual, in which boys demonstrate to each other their sexual potency. The body of the woman becomes merely a vehicle for this. When boys seize upon rape as a ritual, it will not be a passing phenomenon. Just as the tiger becomes addicted to human flesh, so may these young men to the fulfilment of their aggressive drive.

And what of the man? Is it true to say that he continues to practise what he experienced during his rite of passage?

Lest anyone believe that the rites inflicted on young boys of primitive tribes are unimportant to western man, they need only ask any competent film critic. Virtually every serious film ever made features some aspect or other of the male in action, practising those virtues held in such high esteem on the plains of Africa or high on the cliffs of Papua New Guinea. The film makers know all about these rituals. They know that boys cannot dip their spears into the blood of a slain lion, so they provide the experience on celluloid instead. Hollywood is now the high priest of puberty, the circumcisor, the producer of sperm for young men to swallow. Films such as *Top Gun*, *The Young Ones*, *Robin Hood*, *The Magnificent Seven* and thousands more are as popular today as was *The Wild Ones* when it first came out. And as long as boys and men remain what they are, these films and films like them will continue to enthrall. By watching them, a boy can experience, albeit it vicariously, his trial by fire, his mutilation, his feat of heroism and his successful seduction of women. It is no wonder these films are runaway winners. It could be argued that the moguls of American cinema are unconsciously perpetuating what their maleness dictates. They are conscientiously carrying on the functions of the elders of the tribe, the wise men who know instinctively what is needed for the tribe to survive. It is celluloid circumcision.

And it is not only the American film makers who maintain the ritual. Even more fanatical about the rites are the Japanese, whose men will happily kill themselves in a grand one-off show of maleness. For a good account of the Japanese male see the book *Behind the Mask*, by Ian Buruma. Japanese men do not conceal their criteria for manhood beneath a self-deprecatory layer of modesty; not

39

for them the veneer of Hampstead Man. These criteria, traditionally adopted by the Samurai warriors, included bravery to the point of lunacy, unswerving devotion to duty, hard work and loyalty.

The same degree of fanatical adherence to the code of *bushido* was accompanied by no less a fanatical commitment to the enslavement of women. Perhaps there is a cause-effect relationship here.

Interestingly, despite being completely isolated from the West, over the centuries Japanese men have built up a cultural image of themselves not dissimilar from that nurtured in Hollywood, or Paris and London. History, myth and folklore generated exactly the same heroes who ride the big screen.

During the period when Japan began to shake off its feudal origins and become urbanised, petty and organized crime started to increase in the fertile incubators of the cities. Local crooks, swindlers and hard men, including Samurai who had lost their jobs, rampaged, pillaged and stole. Japanese men seized on these piratical types, ascribing to them the qualities of heroes. These tough guys, or *kyokyaku*, as they were called, acquired a legendary status. They subsequently spread into the countryside, roaming around and creating mayhem, and in the process developed the 'Lone Ranger' type of image, which in most cases was entirely inappropriate. The best known and most copied glorification of these bandits was the film *The Seven Samurai*, made by the famous Japanese director Kurosawa. In his book, Buruma cites another example, the first film made by Kurosawa, *Sanshiro Sugata*. The boy, Sanshiro, learns Judo, but although he is proficient, he lacks some indefinable quality of manhood; he has not yet confronted death. Recognizing this deficiency in himself, he asks his tutor's advice. The master simply orders the boy to die. So he throws himself into the water behind a temple and passes the night clinging to a post; if he lets go he drowns. By the time morning comes he has seen the one true way. He has passed his rite of passage.

There is always at least one exception, and the most famous is that of the men of the Polynesian island of Tahiti, who, if anything, have always seemed only too pleased to give away their women to any men who may have stopped by on the islands. They have virtually none of the severe sexual differentiation of roles found virtually everywhere else in the world. Women perform the same roles as men, and women chiefs are not uncommon. There is no pressure on boys to prove their manhood; there are none of the savage rites of passage that boys have to endure in several other societies. Men have no hang-ups about homosexuality, and sleep together whenever they feel like it without any sense of shame or having trangressed some immutable law of nature. Homosexual men practise openly, and are a normal feature of village life. They pluck out their beards and dress and behave as women. These men, or *mahus*, as they are called, offer their services for fellatio or sodomy, and men use them quite freely. The men are not warlike, and will not fight to shield their village or their women. In fact, they have never had to defend their villages or women. The life is certainly easy. Fish are plentiful and there is no need to risk life and limb hunting. Life is peaceful, physical violence the exception rather than the rule, and men rarely if ever take offence.

This may be one of the keys to the tranquillity of this tropical paradise. Tahitians have a poor opinion of anger and aggression. They believe that when one gets angry the emotion should be dissipated through expression and discussion, not by killing and maiming. The statistics are impressive: between 1940 and 1962 there was only one murder.

It sounds as though one were describing human life on

another planet. The factors that produced this type of society should be of great interest to feminists, who see on the island a type of man who poses far less of a threat. A biologist would want to measure the testosterone levels in these men, although presumably they are not insufficient to ensure sexual potency, the masculine shape and fertility. Are their brains any different from those of men elsewhere? Perhaps the biological imperative is not as imperious as the evidence would have us believe. On the other hand, if these men had been removed from Tahiti as babies and transplanted to New York or Tokyo they might have grown up very differently.

Conversely, if a frenetic, hard-nosed commodity dealer were to be shipped off to Tahiti, would he start organising a market in coconut futures, or don a grass skirt and loll about in front of the hut of the local *mahu*? It can be speculated that if environment is important in shaping men's maleness, then a thorough conquest of society by women might result in the pacification of men. This seems unlikely unless we acquire an abundance of fish-filled lagoons and can eradicate all international and national dissent.

Why should a bunch of men have handed authority to women just because their lifestyle was a leisurely affair? Perhaps life was so easy that government seemed like just so much more hard work. Letting the women run things allowed the men to do much more pleasurable things like go fishing. Tahiti certainly raises interesting questions about the effects of the environment on men and has perhaps given us a window through which we can glimpse our own future.

It is, however, a small victory for women. The rest of the world presents a much larger conquest.

The macho male is alive and kicking, except that today he must be content to smell macho, look macho, swagger like a macho man and drive macho cars. He cannot *be* a macho man. In order to be macho, he must go through the rigours of the manhood test. Afterwards, he has to take his place alongside the other men of the village. He must repel raiders, fight injustice, bring home a kill, produce many sons, show great dignity and wisdom. The sex cries of his women must be louder and more sustained that those which issue forth from beneath the bodies of other men. When he speaks other men must fall silent, and when he turns to walk, other men must trot at his heels like dogs.

How many men can do these things today?

Like the Japanese businessman who takes off his suit to don the robes and the Netsuke of the Samurai, or the Texan accountants who once a year peel off their three-piece suits and put on their cowboy gear to join the great trail rides that end in the arena of the rodeo, modern man has two sets of clothing. You may not see him wearing one of them, but that alternative uniform nonetheless hangs in a special cupboard somewhere in his mind. He himself may not know what it looks like. He may never have worn it. But in every man's lifetime he gets at least one glimpse of the uniform, and if he manages to get it on, he will be instantly transformed into the ancient warrior, the Samurai, the Masai, the New Guinea cannibal or the Bedouin, and he will run outside to be worthy of it. He will run straight into women. Women whom he expected to find at home, not running around wearing their own uniforms, or, worse still, his.

There is bound to be conflict. Women have always been a part of man's armaments, the embodiment of his success, the shield he uses against other men. A woman reflects his glory like a mirror. Consider the consequences when he looks into the mirror and sees a woman standing there instead of him. She is supposed to make him shine that much more brightly, not supplant his image. A woman is a goal in a very limited sense. Her orgasm and her babies proclaim his manhood. He has won that accolade in a hard

43

fight, and he is jealous of his success. She is part of a larger image; she is the price tag on his virility. She stands at the end of the painful road to manhood. And even if he never in his life raised so much as a cry, if no whip landed on his back, or no knife sliced through the skin surrounding his glans penis, nevertheless he knows the pain. For he hears the voices of his ancestors. We must not underestimate the potency of the cumulated history of man imprinted in his genes. The hoarse, encouraging cries of the men ring in his ears, and he almost tastes the blood in his mouth. To be confronted by a free woman is an affront.

At a dinner party not long ago I heard a man who works in the media industry say he was worried about the surge of 'anti-men' propaganda, the 'strident, aggressive attacks of the lesbians'. He wasn't worried, he was frightened. He felt threatened, under attack. He emanated fear. What he said was very interesting. It told me a lot about him. Firstly, he didn't really think women should be out there competing with him. Clearly he thought they should be at home taking care of the kids while he toiled away in the real world. Any woman who went to work like a man, and who declared herself an equal verbally or in print was not a 'natural' woman; she had to be a lesbian, an imitator of men (his words). When I described the conditions in Tahiti he reacted scornfully. 'Poofters', (homosexuals) he snorted, 'they can't be made like the rest of us.'

Is he right? All men possess the same numbers of chromosomes and are able to fertilize all women. It is very likely that Tahiti man is fully interchangeable biologically with his Sambian or Yorkshire brother, and that they are all made the same. Let us have a look, then, at how the male is made.

3
To Make a Male

In many human cultures the birth of a boy is greeted with wild joy by the father and relief by the mother. The father has proven to his peers that he can produce a male heir, and the succession of his genes is assured, provided his son survives. His wife remains in favour. If a girl is born the father may smile weakly and go off with his friends to drink off his disappointment. The mother knows she has not pleased her husband. There is therefore much lore about the conditions which will optimize the birth of a male, and not only a male but a good sound male to make a father a proud man. Needless to say all such conditions are of dubious value. Provided nature is left to its own devices the sex of the baby is left to chance. It all depends on the absence or presence of the Y chromosone

Once this has happened, and the sex has been fixed as male, a lot can and does go wrong. Making a male involves some intricately timed events in the developing foetus, including critical changes in brain structure, and these are relatively easily interfered with. Men have put a lot of time and effort into studying the making of the male, and while the main species studied has been the rat, the results nevertheless, have given us a great deal to conjecture with. They have thrown up possible explanations for so-called normal and variant social and sexual behaviour, not only in men but in women, and it is very instructive to follow the development of the male from fertilized egg to full blown adult.

When the adult human male reaches orgasm he

ejaculates about 4 ml (a teaspoonful) of semen high into the vagina near the cervix. Each millilitre contains about 100 million spermatozoa. Potent chemicals in the seminal fluid contract the vaginal muscles strongly on to the penis, and the same chemicals cause contraction of the muscles of the uterus and fallopian tubes, sweeping the spermatozoa upwards to the waiting oocyte or unfertilized egg. The spermatozoon consists of a head, which contains the chromosomes and the enzymes necessary to melt the membranes surrounding the oocyte, a short neck region and a flagellum or tail.

When the spermatozoa cluster around the oocyte their tails lash the head into the right orientation for penetration through the oocyte membrane. One spermatozoon manages to enter the oocyte which immediately becomes sealed off from the others. The spermatozoon loses its tail and the chromosomes of the male and female gametes become combined to form the hybrid cell. This cell, or zygote, divides to form a collection of cells called a morula as it passes down the fallopian tubes to the uterus. About five days after ovulation the mass of cells is now termed a blastocyst which after another three or so days attaches itself to the inner wall of the uterus. Implantation has occurred. The hybrid has taken hold of the host. This is an extraordinary phenomenon because, due to the input of the male's genes, the blastocyst is a foreign body. By rights the female's immune system should reject it, but it does not. Instead the cells of the inner uterine wall or endometrium actually welcome the blastocyst, allowing it to attach itself and to take root and grow. It is the ultimate parasite. How the blastocyst achieves acceptance is unknown, but it may do so by sending chemical signals to the maternal immune system. The blastocyst continues to grow and differentiate into several different layers of cells while a specialized interface called the placenta develops between the mother and the embryo.

Each embryonic cell contains forty-six chromosomes, the genetic database of the individual or phenotype. Two of these are the sex chromosomes which will determine the sex of the embryo. There may be two X chromosomes, in which case the embryo will develop into a female (XX). If, however, there is a Y chromosome, a male will be formed (XY). Note that the X chromosome is present in both sexes. The human body therefore is predisposed to the female form. Initially, the embryo develops rudimentary undifferentiated male and female gonads i.e. testis and ovary, and until the sixth week of pregnancy the embryo is bisexual.

The Y chromosome has a gene, the Y-linked testis-determining gene, which codes for the production of an equally important protein, the H-Y antigen. This protein stimulates the differentiation of the cells of the testis: the seminiferous tubules which will manufacture spermatozoa, and the Leydig cells which produce testosterone, the male sex hormone, when they are formed. Testosterone circulates in the foetus and enters all cells, including the brain. Testosterone stimulates the development of the male sex organs and organizes the formation of a male-type brain.

The female foetus has no Y chromosome and consequently no Leydig cell will develop. In the absence of testosterone, the female genitalia, the vagina, clitoris and hymen will develop, as will the accessory organs, the uterus, fallopian tube and the ovary, which will produce the female sex hormone oestradiol.

As stated above, the embryo is fundamentally female, even if it is XY, unless the male sex hormone testosterone intervenes to masculinize it. This applies also to the brain. From the information we have, it seems likely that the human brain is basically female – unless it is exposed to testosterone at a critical period of its development. In the human foetus the critical period occurs at around six weeks of gestation. This makes it difficult, if not impossible, to study systematically the sexual differentiation of the human brain.

In the case of the rat, however, the situation is different. Unlike the human, the rat's brain is sexually differentiated around the time of birth. The period of gestation for the rat is 21 days, and from about Day 18 of gestation to Day 5 after birth, the rat brain passes through a highly critical period in its development. During this time (Days 18 and 19) the testis of the male foetus starts to produce relatively large amounts of testosterone. The hormone enters the brain and acts to ensure that the rat will grow up to behave like a male. Thus the rat provides a more readily accessible 'window' through which to view brain sexual differentiation.

Sexual behaviour in rats, as in many other species, is differentiated sexually. The adult male rat prefers to mount females. Like almost all mammals, the rat mounts the female from behind. (The human and the pgymy chimpanzee are exceptional in this respect. Male and female copulate facing each other.) The male rat will try to mount females and even other males occasionally and accepts a rebuff equably. Unlike the female, he is always interested in copulation. This is advantageous for the species. She, on the other hand, will accept a male only when she is in oestrus. The reproductive system of an adult female rat operates in a four- to five-day cycle analogous to the menstrual cycle in women. It is not menstrual, however, since the rat does not shed her endometrial lining. There is no bleeding. On the day when she will accept a male i.e. the day of oestrus, she ovulates at around 4 a.m. in the morning. During the early hours of darkness the rats copulate. This makes sense, since they are vulnerable to predators during sexual activity. The sexual differentiation of the male and female is especially apparent at this time. The female indicates her willingness to accept a watching male by wiggling her ears and making short hopping darts in front of him. This is her long sidelong glance. She is showing *proceptivity*. She is proceptive because she finds the male attractive. She would not show proceptivity to another female unless she was attractive. The male is attractive to her not only because of what he does but because he is putting out strong pheromonal signals.

The male then attempts to mount her and she goes into the next phase of behaviour. She indicates her willingness to accept the male by crouching, arching her back in a concave fashion and thrusting her behind into the air. This posture is termed lordosis, a clinical term to describe severe curvature of the spine in humans. In other words she is showing *receptivity*. Once the male has mounted and penetrated, he no longer has any control over his actions. He will reflexly thrust in an attempt to ejaculate. He may not be successful in penetrating or ejaculating at his first attempt. The whole process is very fast. In such a small animal it has to be or the pair can easily be picked off by a passing owl. Unlike the human male, the rat has many small spines on the penis which will aid retention after penetration and presumably stimulate the female more rapidly.

As sexual behaviour goes this is fairly uncomplicated when contrasted with elaborate human foreplay. But the elements are exactly the same: attractiveness, proceptivity and receptivity. These are sexually differentiated, and in the case of the rat this is achieved if testosterone enters the developing brain during the critical period. What happens if it does not?

Whether one likes to hear it or not, there is no doubt that the brains of most, if not all mammals, are sexually differentiated in structure. That is to say, the wiring is different in males and females. In some species, for example the rat, the differences in certain brain areas are so marked that they can be seen with the naked eye on a microscope slide. Furthermore, these differences are linked to differences in sexual behaviour and function. They are, in effect, the fountainhead of gender. These brain areas can be pinpointed. We know a lot about them.

Differences in wiring are also being discovered in the human brain. We don't know what they mean, but we can be reasonably confident that sooner or later scientists will find out, and they will provide irrefutable proof that gender boils down to brain circuitry in very specific areas. What is interesting about all this is that the wiring is apparently not laid down in the chromosomes. Whether you are born genetically XY or XX does not necessarily dictate the wiring that determines gender, or how you perceive your sex.

There is a massive body of evidence which says that the wiring is determined by hormones, the sex hormones, which act on the brain during a critical period of foetal development. If the hormones are not present during the critical period, the animal grows up to think it is a male when it is in fact female, and vice versa.

Without launching into an avalanche of indigestible anatomical detail, it is necessary, however, to outline briefly the brain areas known to be involved in sexual function and behaviour. The brain is divided into three main areas which developed and evolved over millions of years. The most primitive is the spinal cord and hindbrain which control most of the functions needed for survival; these include respiration, circulation, reflexes and control of the digestive system and the heart. They are not significantly involved in sexual function. The midbrain, which developed later in prehistory, is a complex and very poorly understood web of fantastic intricacy which modulates, among other things, muscle movement and wakefulness. Destroy certain areas of the midbrain and one cannot be aroused. The newest part of the brain is the forebrain, which controls appetite, the endocrine system, body temperature, emotion and thought. In fish the forebrain is rudimentary, while in primates it is relatively huge.

The part of the forebrain that interests us is that which lies right at the bottom, just above the roof of the mouth. This is the hypothalamus. It is about 4 g in weight in the adult human – it could fit on a teaspoon. Within its mass of intricate interconnected brain cells, or neurones, are the centres which control appetite, body temperature, water and salt balance, the ejection of milk from the breast and sexual function. It does most of these things because it controls the pituitary gland, with which it is connected through nerve cells and blood vessels. If the connections between the hypothalamus and the pituitary are cut, the animal will survive, although it needs to be given sodium chloride in the diet.

The pituitary gland, under the direction of the brain, releases hormones which drive the testes, ovaries, adrenal glands, thyroid and possibly the thymus. Removal of the pituitary gland causes the testes and ovaries to stop functioning and the animal becomes sterile.

Sexual behaviour is directed by the brain in very specific sites. In animals such as rodents, the area which controls sexual behaviour is situated directly in front of the hypothalamus. It is called the preoptic area, and possibly has the same function in humans. In rats, the preoptic area is very much larger in males than it is in females. What follows is a true story and one as bizarre as any that one is likely to find in nature. It is the way gender may be laid down, and it is guaranteed to give one plenty to think about. It is not anecdotal, but hard evidence, and while rats are not human, much of what has been found in rats applies to human physiology as well.

It was discovered that if female rats were given the male sex hormone testosterone within five days after birth, they grew up to behave sexually like male rats. They tried to mount other rats, male or female, and their pituitaries behaved like male ones. They could not have normal oestrous cycles. When their adult brains were examined, the preoptic area was the same size as that observed in males. What's more, many other brain areas which are different in males and females were of the male pattern. If the hormone was given to the rats at ten days of age, it was not effective. By then, the normal female wiring was permanently in place and could not be tampered with. The critical period for brain sexual differentiation had passed.

Conversely, if a male rat lost its testosterone within five days after birth, it grew up to behave sexually like a female. It lordosed, i.e. it wanted other males to mount it, and it became receptive to other males. Furthermore, its pituitary behaved like a female pituitary, and many other sexually differentiated brain areas resembled those seen in the female. This is corroborated and undisputed information. It also happens in other mammals.

Therefore it can be said with certainty that the male sex hormone intervenes during development of the rodent brain to make irreversible changes in wiring which may underlie changes in gender and sexual function at a basic level. But the plot thickens.

It was also found that the female sex hormone oestradiol was far more potent than was testosterone in changing a neonatal female brain to a male brain. At first this was thought to be a pharmacological effect i.e. artificial, drug-induced and not a reflection of what happens naturally. Not so. It is what happens. In nature, when the male rat is born, and even before, while it is in the uterus, the testis of the male starts secreting testosterone which travels to its brain in its bloodstream. Once there, the brain changes testosterone into oestradiol, which then converts the still female brain into a male brain.

What about other species? It could be argued that this strange action of testosterone is peculiar to the rat and irrelevant to us. In fact, the sexual differentiation of the foetal brain by testosterone has been shown in a number of species, including the mouse, ferret, guinea pig, hamster, dog and sheep. The phenomenon has also been shown in at least one species of fish and in several birds, including the Japanese quail, pigeon, zebra finch and domestic chicken. The brain of the rhesus monkey is also sexually differentiated. The fact that it happens in a primate is of special significance. Anatomists are now finding marked structural differences between different parts of the male and female human brain, although we don't yet know what effects, if any, these differences have on the sexual behaviour, talents, or any other qualities historically attributed to male or female.

The mechanism by which testosterone produces organizational changes in the developing brain of certain species is complex. The nature of the effects is complex also. We can classify some effects of testosterone as 'masculinizing', for example the induction of mounting behaviour. Other effects are termed 'defeminizing'. These include the suppression of the lordosis response. If this did not happen, the male would grow up to show both patterns of sexual behaviour. There is also evidence that in the neonatal female rat some steroid-induced organization is going on, although little is known about this.

We have no information as to whether this occurs in humans. It seems that humans and the other primates have to a great extent been liberated from the chemical straitjacket imposed by the sex hormones on lower orders. The normal human male pituitary can behave like a female pituitary, even though certain brain areas are wired differently in male and female. Human females can become receptive to males at any stage of the menstrual cycle while rats and many other species can only do so during oestrus. At present it's all guesswork. The human foetus brain is sexually differentiated at about six to ten weeks, and doctors are concerned lest women inadvertently continue taking oral contraceptives when pregnant, in case these artificial and very potent oestrogens masculinize the brain of a genetic female. It could be speculated that a male foetus whose testes do not produce enough testosterone to masculinize the brain during the critical period may grow up to be homosexual. On the other hand, gender in the human may be entirely unrelated to this action of testosterone. There is plenty of evidence in other chapters that environmental factors are very important in self-perceived gender.

In humans and in other primates, it may be wrong to think of male and female gender as two entirely separate states. Perhaps gender can be envisaged rather like a ruler with male at one end and female at the other, and the gender of the individual may lie at a particular point on the ruler, that point having been determined by a combination of genetic, hormonal and environmental influences. Those whose brains lie well to one end of the ruler, regardless of their phenotypic sex, might well be the ones who choose their own sex for partners.

Other human attributes, such as the occurrence of learning and perception problems, have been tentatively ascribed to the action of testosterone. It is known, for example, that dyslexia occurs in a significantly greater number of boys than in girls, and it has been speculated that this may be due to the action of testosterone in altering brain laterality. There is, however, no evidence for this elaborate theory.

Finally, all this leads us back to the synthesis of the proto-male by the female. Could it be that she put her oestradiol to use in creating a masculine brain, and that after the proto-male broke away, his testosterone, which made him a male, also took over the function of turning the female brain she had given him into a male brain?

Behavioural scientists find these chemical fireworks

fascinating, but point out, correctly, that other factors also determine how a developing male or female finds his or her gender identity. Let's stay with the rat a while longer. What about social deprivation or stress? Of particular interest is the mother-infant relationship. It is known that the mother rat will spend more time with the male than with the female pups. She licks her offspring, particularly on the anogenital region, and the males get much more licking time than do the females. If, however, the neonatal females are given testosterone, the mother treats them like males. It seems that testosterone produces a stimulus characteristic normally found only in the male, to which the mother responds. If a neonatal male receives insufficient licking he grows up unable to copulate at the same rate as do adequately licked males.

Parental influences are critical even with the newborn. Take the white-crowned sparrow, for example. If an egg is removed from the nest and a male is hatched and reared isolated from other birds, he will not be able to sing the normal adult song. It sounds recognizable but is not quite right. And not only parental but also sibling activity determines the adult behaviour of the male. If a male rat is removed from the litter and reared in isolation, he will grow up knowing that he is supposed to mount a female, but he won't know how to do it. If presented with a female in oestrus, he will climb on her head, her side and her back, but he won't make any progress and he will give up. Similarly, if a male monkey is removed from his mother and reared in isolation, his sexual behaviour when adult will be severely abnormal. A monkey brought up away from his mother is unable to mate. He gets sexually aroused but doesn't know how to mount the female. Like the mother-deprived rat, he tries impossible positions. Interestingly, he can be taught how to do it properly which a rat cannot. This has fascinating possibilities when considering reversibility in brain organization in higher species such as primates. Sex play among human siblings is common, and sexual fantasies by the young involving the parent, therefore, may be positive influences for the determination of normal adult sexual behaviour.

The rat is not alone in showing disparity of attention to male and female siblings. Caged baboons and gorillas pay a lot of attention to the genitalia of their infants, spending much more time examining the genitalia of the male babies. There is definitely a very powerful output from the developing animal, and this too may be sexually differentiated. It sometimes has dramatic connotations. Among bonnet macaque monkeys dominant females are more aggressive to female infants. Rhesus mothers pregnant with daughters are more likely to be attacked and hurt than if they carry sons. Social interactions can even determine the sex of the foetus. A lower ranking female monkey is more likely to have females than males. Clearly the foetus is sexually differentiated for the transmission of signals to the mother and thence to the social group. The fascinating question is whether the response of the group to the mother, or of the mother to the infant after it is born, will alter the development of the latter's brain. In the case of the rat and some birds, there is direct evidence that it does. ·

Stress in the foetus or neonate may also have permanent effects on sexual behaviour, reflecting an irreversible imprinting on developing brain circuitry. It is known that if pregnant rats are stressed for the last five days of gestation, their male offspring will grow up to prefer other males to females, and their behaviour will be feminized i.e. they will lordose for other males. This may be due to an earlier than normal release of testosterone from the foetal testis, resulting in an asynchronous reaction with those developing brain areas which dictate sexual behaviour and preference. It has been suggested that prenatal stress could alter sexual preferences in humans as well. If we are prepared to extrapolate to humans from work with other animals, we can surmise that a woman who is badly and consistently stressed during early pregnancy, when her son's brain is being differentiated for gender, will have a boy who may grow up to be homosexual. The effects of stress on brain development and on ultimate sexual preferences in the human need a lot more study. It is likely that timing is critical in the establishment of male gender, and the interaction of testosterone with specific brain areas at a particular stage of their development is exquisitely timed to achieve this.

The identification of those brain areas would seem to present immense problems. The brain is undoubtedly the most complex organ in the body and its organization reflects this. It is a maze of nerve cells steeped in hundreds of different chemicals, each of which plays a different role. Unlike all the other organs of the body, it is not apparent how the brain is physically arranged to deal with all its different functions. Literally billions of dollars are spent every year on brain research and progress is agonizingly slow. We still don't know how the brain converts a complex electrical circuit into a thought. Until fairly recently it seemed inconceivable that we should be able to point to a small bunch of brain cells and say, with even a small degree of confidence, that these cells might be the spring, the fountainhead of gender, the source of sexual behaviour. The sex hormones, however, have shown us the way and in the rat and monkey brain, at least, brain areas involved in sexual behaviour are now being identified.

Inevitably one wonders just how relevant all this is to us humans. The evidence is interesting.

In most societies women do the cooking and men do the hunting, whether it be hunting a lion or a dollar. Girls play with dolls and boys with guns. Women wear dresses and most men don't. The overwhelming majority of violent crimes are carried out by men. The female rapist is

virtually unknown. These are incontrovertible sex differences in human behaviour. The pressures which brought
them about are interesting, but we must ask ourselves
whether they are determined by testosterone. Is the
wearing of a dress determined by the size of a clump of
nerve cells somewhere in the brain? Is a revolver
programmed into the circuitry?

In humans, there is no evidence that the presence of the
Y chromosome means that a man is destined to behave
differently from a woman. It's more likely that the amount
of testosterone his brain sees during a critical phase of
differentiation may count for much more. By the same
token, a woman's brain may become more 'male' if the
foetus is exposed to unusually high levels of testosterone.
This can and does happen.

Some women suffer from a congenital defect called
congenital adrenal hyperplasia. Their adrenal glands lack
enzymes necessary to produce the steroid hormone
cortisol, and instead they produce androgens. The term
'androgen', incidentally, refers to any substance which acts
like testosterone. This defect manifests itself well before
birth, and these female infants are born with masculinized
genitalia. Their clitoris is enlarged and the labia of the
vagina may be fused. The condition isn't always detected,
and the girls may be raised as boys. But if it is diagnosed
early enough the girls are treated with cortisone. Nevertheless, their brains have been exposed to prenatal
androgen, and the behaviour of several of these girls has
been studied. Basically, as children they behave like
tomboys. They prefer to play with boys and enjoy rough
and tumble games more than do those girls who don't
have the enzyme deficiency. They seem to be less
preoccupied with daydreams of motherhood and marriage, and they aren't all that interested in dolls. They tend
not to focus much on personal adornment and hair.
Nevertheless, they still retain their female gender identity.

When adolescent, they date boys and in due course marry and have children. The retention of gender identity may be in large part due to the fact that their parents treat them like girls and not like boys.

It seems from studies of these girls that there may be two components (at least) which have to be taken into account in the determination of gender. One is organization, and occurs in the uterus; the other is environmental, and depends on the response of the group to the individual. The organizational component is probably irreversible, the environmental influence isn't. Evidence for this comes from South America.

There is in the Dominican Republic a small farming community, some of whose males have a problem. They suffer from a congenital deficiency of an enzyme which converts testosterone into another androgen. This means that their external genitalia are not masculinized before birth. Before the condition attracted clinical interest these boys were thought by their parents to be girls and reared accordingly. They played girls' games and wore dresses. But at about the age of puberty things changed for these 'girls'. Each boy's penis grew, his voice deepened and he developed the normal masculine physique and body hair distribution. The boys were capable of erection and ejaculation from a small orifice situated at the base of the penis. Most of those who were studied switched sex-roles and became men. Many formed bonds with women and lived out their lives as men, although some carried neuroses about their unusual genital anatomy.

This pubertal change happened because these men all have the Y chromosome. Therefore they have testes which at puberty start producing testosterone. The hormone physically masculinizes these boys. But does it influence their behaviour? The answer to this is that it does. It makes them aggressive and boosts their libido (but then testosterone does that to women as well). Since they have a testis, it is likely that their brains were exposed to testosterone in the uterus. One supposes that their brains were masculinized. That, however, does not stop them behaving as girls before puberty.

We have seen how testosterone can have permanent effects on a developing tissue such as the brain. Some of its effects on the adult body, however, are reversible. Testosterone has many effects on the male, and the female. In both sexes it stimulates libido and aggression. It produces the characteristic masculine shape. If a female athlete takes anabolic steroids for any length of time it shows. The hormone stimulates the masculine pattern of hair growth. It promotes acne. A woman with excess testosterone has a bad skin and has hair on her face, arms and chest. These effects are reversed if the hormone is withdrawn. If a man is castrated he changes shape. His muscles soften and he becomes flabby and weak. His penis starts to shrink and he gradually loses interest in using it for sex. He will, however, still be able to copulate, although he will be sterile. His prostate withers. He loses his aggressiveness. The first farmers knew that a castrated bull becomes docile and its flesh is soft and tasty. If, however, man is castrated before puberty, the effects are more marked. He continues to grow because of the continued growth of the long bones. He tends to fatness. His voice remains treble and never breaks. His penis remains small and his prostate does not develop. He does not acquire the typical male hair pattern and won't need to shave. Neither will he go bald. No matter how long he lies in the sun, he will not tan. He is without aggression and has no interest in sex. He does not, however, look like a woman and neither does he turn into one.

All these changes produced by castration can be reversed by treating with testosterone. The male can be turned on or off at will. In this, partly, lies his fragility. But as long as he started off with a Y chromosome, he will develop into a male as we know him, from rat to human.

Generally speaking, men want to be men. They want to be acknowledged as men, and this is possibly the essence of the whole biological conjuring trick that has produced them. This need may be programmed into the neural circuitry, and if it is, it is very bad news for women. Consider the evidence, some of which is anecdotal, but very persuasive for all that. In the first place, the appearance of physical proof of manhood is eagerly awaited by every boy. The first signs of pubic and facial hair are celebrated not only by the boy himself, but by a relieved father, and both parents joyfully guide their son to his manhood.

Boys want not only the more private manifestations of manhood. They passionately want those which proclaim their masculine success to the world. They want height, impressive musculature and the strength that goes with it. This desire for the trappings of manhood is so widespread it is tempting to believe that these feelings are instinctive, part of the proto-male that survive to this day. Certainly, they don't need it in today's world, unless they want to excel in sport. One could even say they're old-fashioned, behind the times. But genetics doesn't follow fashion. Boys will want all the physical trimmings long after society doesn't need them. Conflict is inevitable. Men will need to express their manhood inappropriately. So will boys. Violent crimes among and by male children are increasing.

Child crime could be ascribed to social deprivation, but it could equally reflect the manifestations of the forces that make the male, and make the wrong type of male for the present-day world. It is conceivable that the biological imperative rules and is much more readily expressed in boys than in men. To take the argument even further, it is possible that the biological process of making the male is still going on outside the womb. But out here there are no normal training grounds, no forests in which to run, no small animals to kill with miniature versions of their fathers' weapons, only whatever comes along the pavement. Boys have a low threshold for group violence, which William Golding captured in his famous novel *Lord of the Flies*. A group of well-bred British schoolboys are marooned on a deserted island in the Pacific, and they rapidly establish a ruthless tribal system which tolerates ritual murder and group violence. Golding stripped away the thin veneer that would normally prevent children from reverting to their ancestral origins. It is not unknown for groups of boys to kill a loner, for a resentful son to shoot dead his parents or teacher. In Britain, over 25% of convictions for violent attacks in 1987 were among 10–16 year olds. In 1991, in the London Metropolitan area alone, 14,057 boys between the age of 10–16 were arrested, albeit many for innocuous offences such as vagrancy, compared with 2,827 girls.

If the formative process is going on after birth, it complicates life considerably for the modern male. It means that he has to struggle with the incompatibility between the inexorable processes which make him male and the pressures from society, especially at school, to counteract his dangerous and anachronistic maleness. Those outside influences are dealt with in more detail in Chapter 5. What is particularly relevant here is that a boy's inbuilt biological tutor has reinforcement from his father. Psychologists are unanimous in the view that boys need those inputs from their fathers. Consider, then, what perturbations are lurking out there if fathers are not able to express those formative, nourishing and healthy inputs. If fathers are trying to prove themselves out there in the modern world but cannot do so, they are going to send very distorted messages to their sons, and the consequences could be disastrous for both men and women.

4
Gene Shop

Ask any woman what she wants in a husband, and she may mention intelligence, compassion, strength, patience, wealth and a host of other qualities made virtuous in modern life. But does she really mean it and is she capable of understanding the forces that drive her to a certain man? Is she unwittingly seeking the best male around in view of the fact that she is going to invest so much reproductively in what he has to offer? If studies of other species are anything to go by, she probably is. Men are even less able to pinpoint their criteria for the ideal wife. Their reasoning powers in this respect are clouded by the urge to copulate, and if we look at the courtship behaviour of many other species it may be possible to gain some insight into the factors that determine the choice of mate among humans.

In most species, the sexual behaviour of male and female differs. One sex, often the male, is always on the lookout for an opportunity to copulate. The female, on the other hand, seems content to mate with males of her choosing after which she becomes pregnant and loses interest in sex until she has successfully gestated her young. This is virtually universal in mammals. The reason for the sexual difference is unknown, but may depend on the relative investment made by the parents in the nurturing process. The male may have contributed millions of sperm and that constitutes his investment. The female, on the other hand, has to expend much time and energy on the process of gestation or pregnancy. This is because she produces the larger gamete which remains in her body after fertilization. Therefore she is not in a position to seek another mating until she has given birth to and nurtured her young. The male has no such constraint and wants to copulate. As his partner is not interested he has to seek his sex elsewhere. This puts him into competition with a great many other males who all have the same idea.

Competition among males for the female has been studied in a great many species, not only because such behaviour is interesting in its own right, but hopefully because the results may give us some insight into our own sexual behaviour. Also, it is easier to measure behaviour in other species since the conditions can be to some extent controlled, and the results expressed in statistical data. Human sexual behaviour under normal (or abnormal) living conditions does not lend itself to statistical analysis and so we must turn to other animals in the hope that we shall recognize ourselves on the way.

It should be said that although the male is cast as the hunter, there are in nature instances where it is the female rather than the male who goes a huntin'. The female giant water bug, *Abedus herberti*, notices an attractive male and pesters him until he initiates copulatory activity. She lays her eggs on his back, gluing them in place and leaves him to take care of them. The female sea horse, which is more vivid than the male, swims up to him and displays to attract him. He follows, and when they copulate she is the one to insert her genital papilla into a pouch in his belly where she lays her eggs. Male black grouse cluster together at defined sites, or leks, and posture energetically while the female casts an eye over the talent before making her selection. These are examples of what zoologists call sex role reversal, since it is assumed that in most cases it is the male who initiates the mating process. We distinguish, however, between initiation and selection. It is most often the female who selects her mating partner. I am more concerned here with the male as hunter of the female since he conforms to the proto-male hypothesized in Chapter 1, and also because the human male has chosen to cast himself in this role.

Before launching into an account of the competitive behaviour of the male it is worth pausing a while to consider the concept of competition, which is, after all, a fundamental force in our own society. Competition has been defined as 'the active demand by two or more individuals ... for a common resource'. This definition catches the essence of competition but does not bring home the consequences which can also be defined as a process of elimination. We usually think in terms of winners; yet an important consequence of competition is the elimination of the also-rans. And that is important, especially where sex is concerned, since the male who is fittest will win and his genes will be carried over into the next generation. To put it another way, nobody loves a loser.

Before the male can woo his female he first has to find her. She will help all she can. In the darkness of a warm summer night a female firefly will answer the questing flash of the male with one of her own and thus guide him to her. Furthermore, she will attract only a male of her own species through the distinctive pattern of her flashes. The female mammal calls silently to the male no less effectively, often through odour. The male is able to distinguish the sex, species and even the individual using his nose. The call of the female is irresistible. The message she wafts to him on the air currents or imprints on his retina is guaranteed to produce results. From the moment that the male sucks her smell into his nostrils or gets her into his sights he is drawn into a course of action that will result either in a mating or a retreat.

Humans, too, use odour, although it comes in a bottle and almost certainly drowns out the natural scents that men and women give off as a come-hither. British and

American women bath or shower daily and shave the hair under their armpits. French and Italian women, on the other hand, leave their axillary hair where it is, and perhaps for good reason. If the body is putting out an attractant, there is a good chance that some is emanating from under the arms. It is also highly probable that nothing the perfumers make will match the potency of what comes naturally. But let's assume the message has been received and the male responds.

Happy indeed is the male who finds only the female. The chances are that he will arrive together with several other males or find a male already on the premises. Now he has to make a decision. The lion who comes upon a resident male and his harem sizes up the opposition carefully. If the competition looks formidable he can slink away after a few token snarls and live to love another day or not at all. On the other hand, he may decide to fight, especially if the prize is a large group of fertilizable females. He may have to deal with another male who has designs on the same female. That is competition, and the rampant male has been designed to rise to the challenge, although he is not above seeking help. He who will not fight but gives way before a more powerful male is less likely to perpetuate his genes unless he uses cunning, the so-called sneak approach. More about sneak lovers later.

The male who decides to take on another is putting his life at risk. The fight could be to the death. Chimpanzees, for example, will kill over a female.

Why take a risk? In the case of elephant seals, lions, bison or an 18th-century Turkish prince, the reward for success is a large harem of females. In many other cases, including that of today's human male, the fight is for possession of a single female. The word 'possession' is used deliberately. The male is not fighting necessarily for a female but for an article as well. (Later we shall discover that the attitude of the male to the female alters once he has won her.) There are plenty of females around. Why risk one's life for just one of them? Part of the answer lies with the female herself. The fight often takes place in the presence of the female. Furthermore, it is more than possible that the female will have engineered the fight. A female seal in oestrus, and therefore theoretically happy to copulate with any male, when mounted by a bull will create such a racket that other males will rush to them and a fight will usually result, the victorious bull taking the prize.

The battle itself is going to be as ostentatious as the males can make it. They will strut, bellow and glow if possible. In the case of humans, the male may peek at the female occasionally to see whether she's paying attention. The female is behaving in accordance with Darwin's theory of sexual selection. She's screening the males for the best in genes.

The human male in search of a female faces the same problems in that the more beautiful the female the more competition he has. But unlike the male lion or buffalo, the man is a strategist, and the more ingenious he is the better his chances. No woman is going to be impressed by a man who beats the opposition to a pulp in front of her in the pub, and unless he is a low IQ psychopath he knows it. So he adopts a non-violent approach which can be one of two basic types: the direct approach, and the indirect approach.

The direct approach is the tactic adopted by the less complicated human male. He is generally aware of his assets, be they physical or material, and he flaunts them immediately. In this he has much in common with the strutting male of many other species. His approach is not tailored to the particular requirements of the female he has targeted. He has this in common with the males of other species who have only one routine: they strut their stuff and either it works or it doesn't. He is surprisingly successful.

The indirect approach is peculiar to primates. The male does not show his hand immediately. He may indicate his interest so that the female has no doubts about his intentions (the indirect overt approach), or he will screen his interest until the time to unveil his strategy arrives (the indirect covert approach).

Whether the indirect approach is overt or covert the female recognizes it immediately, and if she is attracted to him, wisely lets him execute it. Whatever his tactics, the male knows only that he has to make a big impression. But no matter what he does, the decision ultimately rests with the female. She is making the big investment and is not prepared to select a poor specimen. This in turn will determine his pattern of behaviour. He is in effect trapped in a dance whose steps are dictated by the female. He seeks a prize, but so does she.

The female is not the only prize. Perhaps of even more importance to him is the attainment of dominance. Possibly what the male really wants is to be top dog, which entails not only getting the pick of the females, but lording it over other males as well.

What is dominance? It can be described as a ranking within a social hierarchy. It defines the right of the individual to resources within a ranked society. In real terms, dominance means power. The male (and it is almost always the male) who dominates, gets what and whom he wants. No wonder the male is prepared to risk his skin for it. Once he has dominance he has not only the female but, more often than not, all the other females as well. It will become clear that in order to win this prize he does not have to overcome the female but the male. In societies where males dominate, the female is an article, part of the package deal. The package may be large or small.

Females may be scattered over a wide area, as in the case of gerbils or voles, or clustered together in regions favourable to nurturing the young. Examples of the latter include elephant seals, bison, baboons and humans. The distribution of the female will dictate the tactics of the male. The male gerbil is polygynous. He will copulate with many females when he can find them. His success rate will depend not on his fighting skills but on his ability to forage for the female – to get there before another male does. His score will be dependent on his skills as a scrambler, not as a fighter. It is unlikely that the gerbil will risk his life for a solitary female – she does not constitute a worthwhile investment. The larger, less mobile polygynous male will need all his powers as a battler. He will also have more incentive to fight. A large group of fertilizable female bison, baboons or seals is worth risking life and limb for, especially when one considers the considerable cost in energy that a large male mammal would have to incur in travelling long distances. Thus, a healthy adult seal will be prepared to take on the resident harem-holder rather than lumber many miles in the hope of finding females.

The instinct to fight and kill can be more powerful than the instinct to survive. This is more often the case under water where instincts are less likely to be overridden by judgement. Consider the male fighting fish.

Near the bank of a river in Thailand a small greenish-grey fish, barely two inches long, patiently builds a bubble nest under an overhang from the shore. He hovers beneath the shimmering cluster and from his mouth he releases the bubbles which bob up and cling to the others. He is the fighting fish, *Betta splendens*, and he bears little resemblance to the gorgeous males which have been bred in captivity.

Another male, dull brown in colour, looms out of the murkiness and they become aware of each other. Instantly both stop swimming. They hang motionless, staring. The fins of each fish swell and glow as the fury rises and suddenly they dart in and crash together in a short, vicious flurry. The nest-builder turns and attacks, his mouth punching into the gills of the other fish. The newcomer backs away, a delicate black thread of blood trailing from a damaged gill. Again they plunge at each other and the wounded fish retires with a torn caudal fin. He has had enough. He turns, swims away and the victor returns to his bubble nest.

He continues to work, ignoring the tear on the side of his mouth where the other fish had gouged him. Night blackens the surface and the male sleeps underneath the dark mass of bubbles.

He wakes to the light and instantly sees a female hovering in the water not far from the nest. Her belly is tightly swollen with eggs. The fins of the male fill with blood and he goes into an attack. She turns to flee and the male is left with a plume from her small caudal fin in his mouth. He returns to the bubble nest and waits beneath it, his fins still aflame.

The battered female watches him for perhaps fifteen minutes. Her fins signal her interest and she swims to station herself under the bubbles and hangs motionless in the water. Her stillness, apart from the gentle movement of her fins, is an invitation to the male. He glides to her and gently wraps his body round hers. They both tremble. They remain in this embrace for a few moments and eggs drift away from the couple. The male releases the female who sinks, seemingly exhausted, into the foliage which rises from the river bottom under the nest. He goes after the eggs which he catches in his mouth and he spits them into the bubble nest. The female returns and the embrace is repeated. Again and again they part and come together.

At length an embrace ceases to yield eggs and the female swims away. The male pursues and thrusts his mouth at her tail, but she avoids him and escapes while snatching up and eating an egg which drifted down from the nest. The male remains under the nest to protect the remaining eggs from predators. Occasionally an eggs falls out of the nest and he retrieves it in his mouth, popping it gently back into the bubbles.

About thirty-five hours later the water immediately below the bubble nest ripples with the quivering of tiny tails. One of the fry falls out of the nest and spirals towards the bottom. The male glides rapidly after it, picks it up and returns it to the nest.

Within six days the fry are free-swimming and the male gives up and swims away into the darkness.

This is a story about two fish whose brains are so small that we should need a microscope to study them at even the most cursory level. It is difficult to believe that the complex, purposive and ultimately successful behaviour of both male and female was the result of considered deliberation. They didn't plan any of it. Their actions were purely reflex and were carried out in a sequence rigidly defined by the genes which dictate the structure of their brains. The male had no say over his response to another male. He didn't have a choice about whether or not to fight. He could no more have backed off than stop breathing. The sight of the other apparently filled each male with a paroxysm of rage and initiated an over-whelming attack response. Put a mirror in front of a male *Betta* and he flares angrily. He may charge his reflection, but his response wanes with successive views of his own image. Other signals are needed to precipitate the full expression of his anger.

On seeing each other their body physiology responded automatically. Hormones were released into the circulation and they dilated the blood vessels to the fins to provide them with extra oxygen for the coming fight. The digestive system shut down and electrical impulses screamed down nerves to the muscles which turned the fish into engines of death. Here truly was naked aggression. They fought, knowing instinctively where to do most damage – ripping fins, tearing at mouth and gills and punching the body over vital organs. The aim was not to frighten or discourage but to kill. Nothing was considered or planned. The concept of mercy was impossible.

Neither fish died. The battered loser did not relinquish the fight through fear. He retired because his injuries stimulated the instinct to survive. He was badly hurt and his brain knew it and triggered a powerful override 'telling' the fish to get the hell out of there. If they had been in a tank where there was no escape he would have been killed. The victor would have finished the job, not through malice but because that is part of the pattern imprinted on the brain of the male.

The male fighting fish successfully defended his bubbles. They were as important to him as is a harem of female red deer to the stag. The red deer is a seasonal breeder. He will mate only in the autumn when his body weight, sperm count and antler size are at their peak. This is not coincidence. The whole package which guarantees male effectiveness has been orchestrated by the changing season acting on the brain to stimulate testis development during the summer. The testes produce the spermatozoa and liberate into the bloodstream the male sex hormone testosterone which produces the physical manifestations of the rutting male and inflames his brain into acts of violence, bloodshed and sex. Castrate a red deer stag and his seasonal breeding behaviour will disappear. The young adult stag, virile and aggressive, is programmed to fight. He is not programmed to plan his tactics thoughtfully and seek allies. Consider, though, the case of the sex-hungry baboon.

A young adult Chacma baboon leaps from rock to rock on the stone-strewn floor of the valley between two towering gorge faces in the Waterberg range of the South African Transvaal. In one hand he clutches a mealie (corn) cob stolen from a nearby farm. His blood is up and he feels confident enough to take on anything or anyone. For some time now he has been following a male and his consort. This has made the target male increasingly irritable and nervous. The challenger sits a little distance from the couple and strips the fibrous coating from the cob. The male sees him and snarls.

The single male sits in the warm sun and considers. He has chosen the indirect overt approach. The female is aware of him and obviously interested. He knows he has several options. He could abandon the take-over attempt, but he is encouraged by the nervousness of the other male. Nevertheless, he doesn't want a fight. He has seen another male ripped from eye to nostril in a similar attempt on the couple and dismisses the idea. He remembers that this female was taken by the present consort after the previous one was shot by a farmer. But the challenger has no intention of waiting for such a stroke of luck. He is content to play a slow war of nerves. He appreciates that he is far more manoeuvrable than his adversary, who has a skittish female to watch as well as him.

The couple move away and he follows at a distance. The male snarls and moves menacingly towards him. The challenger stares back boldly but does not move. The twitchiness of her male has unsettled the female, who occasionally presents her rear to her consort's rival in an unmistakable sign of encouragement.

The challenger's opportunity comes at last when the harassed male is forced to leave his female to drive off another ambitious young adult and the patient rival scampers to the female who turns her back on him. He leaps on to her and thrusts. The tricked male charges them but is halted by the snarl of the challenger and the flash of his fearsome canines. He backs away from the copulating pair and slinks off. He is manifestly deflated. His coat appears ragged, his gait is dispirited and he sits dejectedly at a distance from them, the undisputed loser.

The following morning two older, less dominant males meet each other. They are friends. One male turns and presents his backside to his friend, who gently fondles his genitals. They then face each other and smack their lips energetically while gazing into one another's eyes. The friend immediately reciprocates by turning his back to allow his genitals to be touched.

They move purposefully together towards the successful challenger and his female. On the way they ignore a lone female who presents her rear in a clear invitation to mate. They know exactly whom they want. The younger male watches them and snarls. He has seen these two in action before and knows that his possession of this female will be short-lived. They move in synchronized rhythm, sometimes using identical manoeuvres, coming closer, then moving away. At length one dashes too near for the male's liking and he rushes the older male, his canines bared and his hair standing on end. The other old-timer moves in and mounts the female. His friend moves quickly to the couple and turns to face the usurped male who watches sullenly.

In these exchanges no one was hurt. The emphasis was not on force but on strategy. The male baboon knew he could win the female without a fight. What mattered was brains, not brawn, and the female seemed to have been impressed by the tactics of her various lovers. She did not require a show of brute strength to convince her that a male's genes were worth pairing with her own. We infer that she was selecting for intelligence. She may also have appreciated the potency of a coalition.

Two older, wiser baboon males teamed up to defeat a third without risking their skins. Among baboons it is the older males, not the strongest, who *appear* to copulate the most frequently. This may be because baboons are observed during the day only. Young males might be more active at night when orchestrated team efforts by older males are impossible. Note that the two older animals ignored a female which they could easily have mounted. Successful males seem to know which females are most likely to produce offspring, and they will select these preferentially. That was presumably why the two older males ignored the lone female on their way to harass the target male. Neither would those old-timers have bothered any male who courted a female they did not consider to be a good reproductive bet.

Clearly a single female is a prize worth spending a good deal of time and effort over. Consider then, the attractions of a whole harem. Gelada baboon males keep harems and guard them jealously. Acquiring a harem, therefore, will almost always require a great deal of skill and nerve. (Among gorillas and hamadryas baboons, harems are known to be passed down from father to son.)

A baboon who wants to acquire a harem has several options. He can kidnap a female from someone else's harem and build up his own. This doesn't seem to be a common strategy. He can, on the other hand, risk life and limb and displace the resident male. This does happen, and the displaced male does not leave the harem but stays on as a follower. An aspiring harem-holder may decide to join the group and build up relationships with some of the less favoured females and eventually split off to form his own harem. This tactic isn't without its dangers. The harem-holder will try to drive off his rival and may inflict severe wounds on him. The rival will try to minimize this danger by consorting only with immature females. He may, however, 'go for broke' and attempt to interact with a favoured, mature female. If he does succeed in mounting her, the defeated harem-holder will retire to the fringe of the group. Interestingly, a vanquished male appears to age overnight. His chest patches will wither from brilliant scarlet to the washed-out, pale flesh colour usually seen on juveniles or aged males. Possibly the relegation to a sub-dominant role reduces the secretion of testosterone which normally maintains these vivid chest displays.

What of the male who will not risk a confrontation at any price? There are many examples in nature, from insects to mammals, of males who will not openly compete with other males for the female, but use covert strategies in the hope of winning a copulation. There are the so-called 'sneak' fertilizers. Among red deer there are males, called hummels, which never grow antlers. Not surprisingly they will not fight other males. Certain fish are sneak fertilizers, and resemble the female more than the male. In a pond full of large, fearsome male bullfrogs croaking their hearts out to attract a female, a smaller male may hide in the mud and jump on a female on her way to one of the big croakers. The sneak lover may simply be a neurotic male intent on giving the appearance that he is successful with females. Among rhesus monkeys, it is only the dominant males who gain access to fertile females during the breeding season. One does, however, observe other, lower ranking males behaving furtively, if unsuccessfully. It is all a big act, but perhaps understandable when one knows that rhesus monkeys will kill to attain dominance, and will deliberately slash at an opponent's scrotum. The subordinate male chimpanzee is only too aware of the risks. A male has been observed to get an erection on seeing a female in heat, only to hide his erection behind his hands when a dominant male ambled by.

Among humans one also encounters the male who gives the impression that he copulates often. He starts his fantasies young, usually in the playground. He boasts to other boys about his conquests, usually with older women who are friends of his mother. He tells a good story and often goes on to believe it himself, becoming highly indignant on meeting scepticism. As an adolescent and young adult he obtains his pleasure vicariously. He is likely to be a virgin, fearful of the aggression required to court the female in competition. Instead he courts the favour of other males by 'fixing' them up with girls or women. He is the unpaid pimp.

Clearly then, the human male has come a long way from the blind fury of the male fighting fish, from the proto-male who scoured the land for indiscriminate courtships. He will not initiate courtship with any female, only with those who attract him. The extent of his courtship and the intensity with which he pursues the female are dictated by imponderables. But it is clear that those factors can be virtually as imperative as those which are laid down in the genes in other species. They can drive the male to a prolonged, single-minded courtship, and the investment he puts into it is directly related to his expectations from it. Thus, a complication arises. He is still the male who will not be denied, and the female who has permitted a long courtship may have placed herself in danger if for any reason she halts the courtship process. She is interrupting something that has virtually become a ritual for the male. One assumes that his motive is the formation of a permanent pair-bond, but it might simply be the attainment of sexual intercourse with the female.

The human female, too, may initiate and attempt to sustain a courtship. She may elaborate and carry out a plan to win the male, and her aim is usually to establish a long-term relationship. She, however, is dealing with the human male, also seems to want a pair-bond, but only for as long as it takes to transfer his genes.

There is little doubt that both male and female human are capable of very strong emotional attachments, and these are not linked to or dependent on any ritual and response, since the attachment may be one-sided and not reciprocated. Unlike the male rat or baboon, who will shrug off an unsuccessful copulation attempt, and look for another female, the human, especially the human male, will react to a rejection with an intensification of effort. This, too, is a potential source of danger for the female as her rejection might kindle aggression in the male which, in turn, may cause him to seek copulation by force.

And what of copulation? Poets would have us believe it is the summit of love, the ultimate expression of the highest emotion. Perhaps it is. But one finds little evidence of affection when contemplating a female praying mantis devouring the male during copulation.

Strictly speaking, copulation has one function only: to ensure that sperm are successfully transferred from the male to the female. But clearly it is more than that for many species. It is a process which in human males and females, at least, culminates in a paroxysm of emotion that is virtually beyond verbal description. We can only surmise that it is experienced by many other species since the male seeks it so avidly, and will attempt to experience it whenever he can, even without gaining the consent of the female.

Copulation is probably the most dangerous activity for any creature. During the process both partners are vulnerable to attack by predators or from each other. The act itself can be ferocious. Frequently animals will growl or scream during copulation. The males of many species will grip the throat of the female in their jaws; she is very close to extinction. A tom will seize the neck of the female cat tightly in his mouth and it is not uncommon for her to give a piercing or wailing cry. It is not surprising, therefore, that the female wants to see a clearly recognized behavioural sequence from the male before she will let him get near her.

Human copulation is the closest any two people can get to each other. In fact they get right inside each other. This is a very risky thing to do, to allow another human being to get so close when you know that at some point during copulation you are going to lose control completely and would be unable to resist a lover turned killer. And even if he or she isn't intent on killing you deliberately, you could be left with a more prolonged death through AIDS.

Some men and women view copulation as a violent act, and use it both in fantasy and reality to free themselves temporarily from the restraints of everyday life. The violence may be verbal only, but it is no less violent for that. It is also apparently completely out of character for those who do it. There is no adequate explanation for the transition from dignified male to slavering beast as can occur in the bedroom at night. A caring and considerate husband who wouldn't dream of swearing in front of other women will climb onto a bed with his wife and slam his body against hers. He will call his wife the most humiliating and degrading names he can think of and often will demand that she take on the role of whore in order to heighten his pleasure. He will cajole or force her to accept intercourse through her anus or orally. He may want to hurt her or to be hurt himself in order to gain sexual climax. He may need to put on fancy dress. The variations are as varied as the human imagination.

It seems that copulation is an opportunity for some men to do all the things they wouldn't dare to do outside: it is an arena where dreams of dominance can be acted out without the danger of crossing a more dominant male. It is a woman's hard luck that she happens to be there as well when he does it. Sometimes it is fatal for her.

Advanced behaviour, socialization into groups and co-operative behaviour are all very well, but they can turn the female's life into a nightmare. When a female chimpanzee becomes receptive the males pick it up immediately. It's a throwback to the rigid days of stereotyped courtship. The enthusiastic males will surround her boisterously and she may well end up copulating with as many as twenty males. Among orang-utans in the wild, any female is potentially a rape victim. There is no courtship here. No consent, no elaborate ritual. A female, even one newly arrived, will be raped, even by sub-adult males. Usually, however, it is the highest ranking male who carries out the rape.

What has happened to all the safeguards? The system has broken down. And it is the female, and not the male, who is at risk.

In no species has the system broken down more completely than in that of the modern human.

Consider human male group behaviour. When Marilyn Monroe was airlifted to the American troops in Korea in 1954, there was a near riot. When the British pin-up Samantha Fox stood before an audience of Irishmen in 1986 the men stormed her in a frenzy and she had to be rushed away for her own safety. Their behaviour can be compared to that of the sperm which they were presumably so keen to liberate into her body. Many male individuals (sperm) attack the female (ovum) but only one would succeed in penetrating. There may be a recognizable evolutional link between the parts and the whole.

Would these men have forced copulation on the women? One doesn't know. One thing is certain. Those males made the courtship move usually seen immediately prior to intercourse: they tried to touch the female. They were very close to their origins. They were not carrying out considered behaviour. Their action could be described virtually as reflex. A sort of preamble to rape – courtship gone wrong. One might be forgiven for thinking that rape is a price of evolution. But it is not necessarily the case.

If one member shows an interest, is not encouraged but persists nevertheless, and succeeds in coupling forcibly, this is rape. It is difficult to find an instance in nature where females rape males. On the other hand, there are examples from insects all the way up to the primates of the rape of the female by the male.

The male black-tipped hangingfly hangs delicately from a twig near the floor of a cool forest. He resembles a dragonfly. He has caught a fly but does not feed on it.

Instead he everts his abdominal glands and secretes a powerful chemical which is carried away in the air currents. This chemical is a pheromone, an air-borne message to any females in the vicinity. Before long, a female glides in on gossamer wings and hangs close to him. The male holds out the fly which she grasps *but he does not let go*. She starts feeding and he immediately starts copulating. If she eats it all before the twenty minutes required for sperm transfer she breaks off copulation and flies away. If he completes copulation before she has polished off the fly he drives her off and keeps the remains for the next female.

This is a tough trade. We call it prostitution. It is impossible to know whether the female enjoyed copulation while feeding. As a rough approximation, try eating an apple while making love.

The scorpionfly, a close relation, has a similar strategy. But if he cannot catch an insect, his mouth literally waters until he has prepared a relatively enormous salivary mass which is highly nutritious. The female drops down to eat the offering while the male copulates. But cooking up this treat is highly debilitating for the male, who may simply reach up and pull down a passing female and attempt copulation by force. This is rape. The female resists the rapist male and attempts to flee. But if the male succeeds in copulating it is unlikely that the mating will be fertile. Somehow the female prevents fertilization. It is a fact that male scorpionflies prefer to offer the female an arthropod or a lump of saliva, and use rape as a last resort.

On a fine spring day you might admire the aerial acrobatics of a group of bank swallows. You could well be watching an attempted rape. A male whose mate has successfully produced a complete clutch of eggs will take to the air in search of sex. If he sees a male escorting his mate in the air he may try to evade the male, knock the female out of the air and attempt to force himself on her.

Invariably she will resist. Interestingly, the rapist male is highly selective, targeting those females which are still laying. I have already mentioned the gang rape of a duck by several drakes. Some scientists shy away from the term 'rape', since we can't be sure if the female is really unwilling. How about 'forced extrapair copulation' (not my invention)? This problem isn't confined to bank swallows. It seems to be common among monogamous birds such as gulls, herons and the albatross. Notice that it's the males and not the females who fly off in search of sex. Is it because the females are too busy laying eggs or because they're simply not interested in someone else's mate?

It appears that there are only two species of primates which practise rape: orang-utans and humans. The orang male will rape unwilling females while the human male will rape either sex. With orangs it seems that conception occurs only if the female consents.

The human rapist is still a mystery. His motives are not clear-cut, not even to himself. It is not simply an orgasm he is after. He could achieve that by masturbation. He does not seek a partner; he could purchase a willing consort, male or female. Furthermore, many rapists are actually married and copulating regularly with their wives. It is possible that the rapist is frustrated through vocational failure. Often he is subordinate at work or inefficient. But then so are many other men who do not wander out in order to rape women. It has been argued that rape is the male's way of preserving his genes. This seems unlikely. I have already cited examples that suggest the female can prevent conception after rape. Human rapists often kill their victims, thus extinguishing their own forcibly injected genes. The rapist not only assaults the female sexually but often abuses her verbally. The aim, it seems, it to show her that she is subordinate to him: weaker than he is and helpless in his presence. It is not unknown for the rapist to defecate on her.

Is there something biologically wrong with the rapist? Is he a mentally ill person whose condition might be amenable to treatment? There have been some studies of male sex offenders, and the most violent were found to have higher testosterone levels than other rapists, but this seems too facile an explanation for rape. It is more likely that every human male is potentially a rapist with inter-individual variation in threshold for action. In other words, some find it easier than others. In yet other words, rape is not rape in the mind of the rapist. Many rapists have been questioned about their motives: their reasons for attack are to inspire fear, to show contempt, to wreak revenge, to exert power. In other words, no rapist is primarily interested in sex.

In the good old days man was the hunter and women the prey. When he found her he sought signs of proceptivity and if she gave him the come-on they mated to mutual satisfaction. In all probability they formed a pair-bond and he didn't allow any other males near her. From this sprung the phenomenon of jealousy. He would have been stunned had she sent encouraging signals and then turned him down i.e. if she showed him proceptivity but not receptivity. It's likely that he would have raped her. Not much has changed since those far-off times. The male still looks for encouraging signs and is shocked when he realizes it is not proceptivity but simply the fashion of the day or just plain friendliness.

Rape is the fastest growing crime in North America, and is on the increase in Europe as well. Something is happening in the mind of the human male, and it bodes ill for the female. Basically the male is out of touch. He has been built for a number of functions, most of which he can no longer carry out. He is a hunter and a killer and he is not allowed to do either. He is promiscuous, but society has ruled that he is allowed one mate only. Furthermore, the female is actively changing her role, in fact adopting many functions he has considered to be exclusively his. She does not respond to his signals and his opportunities for copulation are limited. On top of that, changes may be taking place in his brain, and possibly in that of the female, to diminish sexual differences between them, and the consequences of those changes are at present not known.

Whatever they are, they may be contributing to a conflict in the human male brain that precipitates the attack on the female. As stated above, motives for rape vary. Attempts have been made to classify various 'types' of rapist. There is the man who finds it impossible to initiate or succeed in courtship. He therefore bypasses it and moves directly to intercourse. In his case, at least, the dominant motive seems to be sex. He is likely to expose himself to women (which could be construed as threatening behaviour). He is akin to the sneak lover, the frog who lies in wait for the female who is attracted to a larger and more tempting male, the deer without antlers. He is the boy who suffered bullying at school, and was driven undercover. He will make obscene calls, even as a child, and attempt to look up a girl's dress surreptitiously. Peter Sutcliffe, the man they called the Yorkshire Ripper, falls loosely into this category. He tried at times to chat up his victims, and on at least one occasion, followed the woman when she didn't respond, hit her on the head with a hammer and raped her. He mutilated his victims, but his main intention was to silence them forever. He targeted prostitutes mainly, not through hatred but because they were easy meat, and less likely, he thought, to arouse public outrage. But he didn't kill only prostitutes. A schoolgirl who was attacked with a hammer and who survived, gave a very good description of Sutcliffe, although he was not charged with this crime. He also attacked and killed a Bradford University student.

Then there is the rapist who is motivated by anger. He is more dominant than the sneak lover. He may even be attractive to women, and use this for conventional courtship. But his courtship ritual is polluted by a damaging relationship with one or more women, which probably occurred early in life. He lives on a short fuse, as far as women are concerned, losing his temper easily and becoming verbally abusive. But he will rarely, if ever, attack the object of his fury, usually his mate. Instead he will plan an attack, picking up a woman in a pub, for example, initiating what appears to be sincere courtship, and then raping her, usually with violence. He laces his revenge by humiliating his victim. He is likely to kill her in his fury, and also to remove the only witness. There does not seem to be any counterpart to him in any other species.

Another exclusively human type of rapist is the so-called sadistic rapist, whose motive is self-evident. He wants to hurt his victim, and he may also wish to inflict pain on a willing sexual partner.

Marital rape is now a crime in England. It has been a crime in Scotland since 1989. But passing a law does not change male behaviour. Men will continue to rape their wives. A man who rapes his wife considers that she owes him access to her body. He takes what he feels is his by right. He has won this woman in the meat markets of courtship, and he is entitled to take his pleasure since he has provided the woman with shelter. But more than that, he is hiding behind a curtain of anonymity and shame. His anonymity and her shame. He knows that his wife is unlikely to report him to the police, even if she can prove it. In the first place, his next attack will be more violent, even if she is separated from him. Secondly, she does not think she will be believed, although in this she is wrong, since police attitudes to domestic violence are moving towards active intervention. Thirdly, if it does go to court, it will be damnably difficult to prove. In fact, she might be better off accusing him of assault, which the courts find less difficult to cope with.

There is another, and very sinister use of rape, exemplified by a well-publicized, recent case in Pakistan. Farhana Hayat is the daughter of Sardar Shaukat Hayat Khan, leader of the Khattar clan, and one of the signatories to the founding of Pakistan. Farhana, who runs one of the most fashionable boutiques in Karachi, had, like her good friend Ms Benazir Bhutto, liberated herself from the tight constraints normally placed on women by the male-dominated society of Pakistan. She owns her own house, is divorced, and to all intents and purposes had shaken off the shackles that appear to lie so heavily on Islamic women. Her freedom may have cost her dear.

In December, 1991, four men broke into her villa and gang-raped her while quizzing her on her friendship with Ms Bhutto. Her father suspected the secret police, whom he thought were ordered to her house by the President of Pakistan's son-in-law, who at that time was the Home Minister for the Sind Province.

While this may be a purely political act, it does shed light on the attitude of men in some countries to the movement towards freedom of their wives and daughters. Presumably these rapists, who would be driven insensate with rage at an inviolation of their own women, have experienced a lowering of their threshold for violence towards women who have moved nearer to behaving like men.

Rape inevitably affects women's position in society. It restricts them. No longer is it safe to go out for a walk in a lonely place, even in daylight. Women are raped when they consider themselves to be relatively safe. A survey carried out by the British magazine *Company* reported that 10% of women questioned had been raped or sexually attacked in 1990. Most women interviewed felt unsafe on the London Underground despite increased Transport Police activity, and almost half had been followed by men or been the victims of flashers. Virtually all the women expressed fears about going out after dark, wherever they lived. After interviewing 3000 women in Britain, *She* magazine published a survey in November 1992 reporting that half the women interviewed had received an obscene phone call, and a third were victims of indecent exposure. About one tenth had been sexually assaulted or attacked by men.

The life of a woman today is polluted by fear. A woman who drives on the motorway fears a breakdown more than any man does. Whether parked in the car waiting for assistance or walking to the telephone, women have been attacked, raped and sometimes murdered. Males intent on rape have even forced women drivers off the road and broken into their motor cars.

This is predatory behaviour. These men are not acting on a whim. They are executing a planned manoeuvre, possibly after selecting and following a victim for many miles. The motorway rapist is a hunter. If placed in his ancestral hunting grounds he would not be in the forefront of a hue and cry after a dangerous animal, but lurking in the rearguard, waiting for the animal to be mortally wounded before rushing in, screaming, with his spear.

Women, understandably, are arming themselves. According to the *Company* survey, one in ten women are starting to carry weapons. In America, many drivers now travel with a revolver or automatic pistol in the glove compartment. They carry anti-personnel equipment such as mace sprays or electric stun guns. These weapons are illegal in Britain, but some women will obtain them nevertheless. Since rape and violent attacks on women are likely to increase in frequency the problem will escalate, and we will witness a greater number of bloody confrontations between men and women as well.

An American film called *Thelma and Louise*, starring Susan Sarandon and Geena Davis, profiles two armed women who are prepared to use their weapons. When a predatory married man tries to rape Davis in a car park, Sarandon shoots him dead. They go on the run, and humiliate and threaten various men who try to stop them. Inevitably, however, the law in the shape of hundreds of (male) police corner them at the edge of a canyon. They choose to stay wild and drive themselves over the edge into the abyss. The film sums up the frustration of American women, particularly those in the southern United States, and the inevitability of the male victory with his superior firepower.

Violence against women isn't confined to direct physical attack. Many men who fear the confrontation will hide behind the veil of anonymity. These are the sneak lovers, the undersized toads. They get their kicks at one end of the telephone. Their effects on women, for it is almost always women who get obscene calls, can be devastating. Yet many insist that they wouldn't dream of assaulting a woman. In a recent case, a man was charged with indecent behaviour for making obscene phone calls during which he terrified strange women so much that they undressed at his command. In *Women, Men and Rape*, Wyre and Swift list the motives given by obscene callers. These range from the desire for kicks, sexual excitement (when the caller may masturbate during or after the call) to exacting revenge on women, or hurting them: the angry or sadistic rape by proxy.

Whatever the reason for making the call, most obscene callers want the same basic thing: they want the call to progress from an introduction to more sexually explicit details. They want the woman at the other end to enter into the spirit of the thing, either by a fearful or a lustful response. The obscene caller is often under the delusion that women are turned on by 'dirty' talk. The biggest turnoff, according to Wyre and Swift, is to put down the phone immediately. The caller usually moves on to another number.

There is little doubt that men and women are being manoeuvred by events to face each other on the battlefield. Both in the media and in the streets, men and women are dying at each other's hands, and if trends are anything to go by, it is going to get worse. Women are prepared to fight, but they are still no match for the male hunter, who is physically stronger and at present better armed. If anything, their resistance might make the fight more spicy for him. The human male may have lost his opportunities to hunt and kill other species. But he has discovered a large population of fairly defenceless and readily available prey in order to slake his thirst for blood. And that prey is the human female.

He has to be taught from an early age that for the safety of the species women must not be included among his prey.

5

Learning to be Superior

A teacher in a London primary school asked her class of 11-year-olds to write an essay. She gave them a choice between two titles: 'A visit to my Granny', or 'The Leader'. All the boys chose the latter topic, and all the girls chose the former. The teacher made no suggestions and the children did not discuss their choice of essay title before they started writing. This modest experiment produced a result which shows that little boys and girls think very differently about certain aspects of life.

That statement might be inflammatory to many people, but it is true nonetheless, and in this chapter many examples will bear out its validity. What is *not* claimed here, however, is that this sex difference in thought and attitude is genetically determined. Even so, that possibility exists, and is fiercely debated. There is a great deal of evidence that children are taught at home, at school, at play and at university to think according to their genetic sex, and there is no evidence that this master plan for producing adult men and women has changed to any significant extent, despite the efforts of the Women's Movement. Nature or nurture; which is it, and can anything be done to change attitudes? More importantly, is there a will?

The nature versus nurture theory takes up a lot of paper and time, and people can't agree about the relative importance of genetic imprinting and learning. With regard to the development of gender identity, the controversy is particularly confusing. There are those who swear blind that males are born to pin-striped suits and the boardroom, while females are doomed by their chromosomes to a life in the scullery. This assertion is based mainly on observations of other species, and of men and women's behaviour through history. But those who have actually gone into the home, nursery and classroom have come away with evidence that from a very early age boys are groomed to think they are the superior sex. How did they learn this?

One might be forgiven for thinking their teachers are other males. After all, men have a vested interest in perpetuating the myth. Fathers who have sweated away their lives building up a small, medium or large material empire want to think it will be left in safe, strong hands, hopefully those of a worthy son and heir. Therefore they will be anxious to ensure that from an early age their sons are taught how to be tough, decisive and unafraid.

Successful modern men are no less concerned than were their forefathers that their sons should grow into warriors and hunters. But they are too busy to attend personally to the inculcation of their boys with the necessary predatory qualities. So they look to educational institutions to provide the right milieu in which a steady, reliable pool of young bulls can be nurtured. Who better to teach these qualities, or help to bring them out but other men. And indeed in some societies, particularly primitive ones, boys are removed from their homes at a certain age and handed over to men of the tribe who will teach them how to be men. This sexual difference in nurturing was practised in relatively sophisticated cultures from way back, for example in ancient Sparta. In Britain there is an attenuated example of this primitive practice in the form of the elitist boys' and girls' public schools in which boys are taught mainly by men and girls are taught by women. But in most western societies boys and girls sit side by side in class. And if we look at the sex of the teachers whose influence will be greatest in determining gender identity, we find that in the main they are female. And this doesn't apply only to humans. How much time do males spend with their young? Let's have a quick look at some other species.

Among certain forms of life, parental care is minimal or non-existent. Many parents will never know their young at all. It is unlikely that most species of fish, snakes, turtles and aphids would recognize their own offspring if they bumped into each other in bright sunlight. It has to be concluded, therefore, that the males of those species are not taught to behave like males. Yet they grow up to behave and possibly think like males. It's all enshrined in the genes. They are tightly locked into maleness, and there seems to be no possibility that they have any choice. They do not deviate from their chromosomally determined sex. We cannot say anything about their attitude to the female, assuming they have one.

Certain males will never look after their young. The male Canadian salmon dies, exhausted, after fertilizing the 3000–5000 eggs his mate has laid. She, too, is killed by her reproductive effort. Neither fish was in good condition anyway, having battled miles upstream to their spawning ground. This is semelparity, or self-destruct reproduction. The male salmon isn't the only species to die of parenthood.

In Australia there lives the small nocturnal marsupial, *Antichinus stuartii*. The males of this species copulate with the females, and when the females fall pregnant the males all die within three weeks of mating. Since pregnancy lasts around four weeks, the males never see their offspring. Females, on the other hand, live to breed again.

Many species of father, however, are involved to a greater or lesser extent in the raising of their young. This can last a few days, as we have already seen in the case of the fighting fish, or for many years, as in the case of the human. And the degree of commitment can be quite awesome, even if short-lived.

The male grey-faced petrel will sit on a single egg for seventeen days while his mate flies over 600 km to the nearest fishing grounds. When she returns, she sits while he flies off for a meal. Thus they alternate until the chick hatches out after an incubation period of fifty-five days. They time things pretty well too; the female arrives back just in time for the hatching. She regurgitates food for the chick, who might otherwise have had to wait days for its first meal. Both male and female rear the chick for four months until it takes off on its own. This is a good example of devoted synchronised cooperation between male and female parents to maximise the chances of successfully raising a single offspring.

Examples of what we call biparental care are far less common among mammals. It is rare to find a male who shares in his mate's maternal duties. More commonly, males and females have different parental roles. The female is more likely to be the direct carer, nursing, holding, feeding and grooming her young. The male is the indirect carer. He finds shelter, roams far afield to obtain food, protects his family, and may assist his male offspring to obtain a mate.

The female invests much more time and energy in infant care than does the male. The male is usually too far away to be of much help, especially if he is a wild carnivore. But even if the male stays close to home he may still pay little attention to the rearing of his young. Witness, for example, the lumbering male elephant seal who will squash to death one or more of his young in his eagerness to mount the female. One supposes that he doesn't care, even though he is certain the young are his.

After studying the behaviour of many male mammals, one is forced to conclude that their young offspring do not get much attention from them. So it is unlikely that the fathers teach them how to be a male or how to behave towards the female. So who does? Of course we know very little about how animals of other species communicate with each other, and it is possible that a great deal of teaching and learning does go on in these families. But if the young, for example ducklings or cygnets, are learning gender identity from their parents, they must surely be primed genetically at a very fundamental level to absorb and reproduce appropriate behaviour patterns, a situation vastly different from the complex discriminatory learning abilities of the primates, especially those of the human child.

In the case of the other primates we have no idea how the male views the female. We shall probably never know if he worships the ground she walks on, is tortured with homicidal jealousy or regards her as inferior in any way. There is very little doubt, however, that the human male has definite views about the role of the female. Most importantly, he views her role biologically and socially as different from his own. Here is a list of statements made by men, women, girls and boys who were asked what they thought about sharing role-duties and play, and about prospects:

A construction worker: 'Ain't natural. If God had wanted women to make buildings he'd have given 'em muscles, wouldn't he?'

Boy of ten: 'Girls can't do what we do. They don't have the brains. Anyway, they're silly and just giggle.'

Housewife: 'Personally, I'm glad to let them go out there and tear each other to pieces, dear. It's much safer at home.'

Male doctor: 'We've opened Pandora's box, mate.'

Girl of fifteen: 'My mum ended up in the kitchen all her life, and I expect I'll end up there too. Like she says, men have got it all, haven't they?'

Sixteen-year-old boy: 'Thank God I'm not a girl, having to worry about rape and all that shit. I feel really sorry for them. But that's life, isn't it. I mean, women make babies, don't they? How can they expect anything else.'

Eighteen-year-old girl: 'I don't go round feeling their bums at work. I wish they'd keep their hands to themselves.'

Playschool teacher: 'By the time they get here they know what's expected of them. They already know how to be boys and girls.'

Indeed they do. Boys, particularly, have very strong ideas about the image they are meant to project. They also know, or think they know, how to view girls.

Humans are one of the few species to nurse their offspring all the way up to adulthood. And there is a great deal of evidence to show that it is during this period that the male learns to be superior and girls are taught to be mere females. A boy's initial schooling is at home, and what he learns there is reinforced when he goes to school and at other centres of socialization within the male child's cultural environment. Let's look more closely at the parents themselves, especially the father.

From birth onwards, from the point when parents first learn the sex of their offspring, their behaviour towards their child is dictated by its sex. Boys will be given boys' toys and girls will get dolls, dollhouses and pink wallpaper. From the word go, boys are shown how to behave differently from girls. As they grow older, they will receive parental rewards for behaviour appropriate to their gender, and they will be punished for aberrant behaviour. Parents unwittingly initiate sex typing of their babies. They have strong ideas about gender and appearance. Both men and women will describe newborn girls as 'softer', having finer features, and being less attentive than baby boys, despite studies which do not find these physical sex differences between infant boys and girls. Women with babies of their own have been presented with six-month-old baby boys dressed as girls and vice versa. When they thought the babies were boys they reacted to them with physical play, whereas those they assumed to be girls were soothed and comforted in an entirely different way. Fathers, too, respond differently according to perceived sex. In fact, fathers will play preferentially with sons rather than with daughters. And this parental preference for a male offspring probably manifests itself as soon as the father learns the sex of his new baby. Thus from a very early point there is pressure on the child to fulfil the gender identity demands made by others.

There is more pressure on boys to conform than there is on girls. This is an important point; it may help in understanding why boys consider that they have to dominate girls. The fact is that there is more pressure on boys to behave like boys than there is on girls to behave like girls. The daughter who enjoys boys' rough-and-tumble play is labelled a tom-boy and nobody minds very much. She'll grow out of it, they say fondly. But a boy who likes to play with dolls, who behaves like a girl and becomes labelled a sissie is likely to be punished by a father who fears he has spawned a homosexual. The father feels that his son will lack power and status in a tough man's world. Thus boys tend to suffer more punishment than do girls. Also, fathers, particularly those who have not come up to their own expectations in life, may transfer those ambitions to their sons. Very rarely, however, do they so burden their daughters. Their son will be rich, rise to the top of their profession, win the Nobel Prize or even become prime minister or president. Not only do fathers transfer these dreams, they make them known to the children, sometimes in subtle, but nonetheless, unmistakable ways. This tactic places heavy pressure on sons to fulfil their father's expectations. Young boys worship their fathers, and it is usually during this period of uncritical adulation that fathers strike. Boys therefore walk around from a relatively early age carrying a burden of responsibility, real or imagined, towards their fathers.

Girls, on the other hand, often have a different battle on their hands. Their fathers may want the exact opposite for them. We have already seen that in primitive (and not so primitive) societies, men view their women as property, and guard them jealously. Daughters in these societies are constrained from a very early age. They may never have the company of a boy until they are introduced by their parents to the man they are going to marry. Fathers ensure that their daughters are hidden away, but they leave their education to the women.

In western societies this rigid educational stricture has all but disappeared. Daughters are free to go to school, play with boys and girls, and are free to choose their own profession. But until their late teens they are still under the influence of a less overtly jealous male parent, but a jealous male nevertheless. Many fathers secretly disapprove of their independent, at times pushy daughters who seem to have picked up many of the ways and ideas of their brothers. Modern western fathers have backed away from confrontation with their daughters, but they have not given up the fight.

This stereotyping of gender is reinforced by the children themselves within their own peer groups. A three-year-old boy who expressed a desire to make a meal was told by a little girl that 'daddies don't cook'. Three to four-year-old children are unlikely to initiate play with other children if the game involves opposite gender activity. We have to ask whether this comes naturally or whether their play is basically in imitation of their parents. Girls tend to play in small groups, often in pairs; girls place very high value on 'best friends'. Their play is non-competitive and coopera- tive. They don't cope well with quarrels, which easily break up the group. As if to steer clear of this danger, girls at play criticize carefully and subtly. They listen carefully, confide willingly and interpret correctly.

Boys play together very differently. They organize their play, but in larger groups. Not for them the cosy intimacy of a confidence, but the loud proclamation of self, the young male rampant. They will be loud and individualistic, full of posture and bombast. The aim is not to share but to take; to take the respect of the other boys if they can: to take leadership; to rule. Speech is directed to these ends.

Boys don't like naked aggression which could result in injury, and differences are quickly patched up. The threat is generally considered enough. Physical aggression for its own sake is feared and the bully is avoided and shunned. Boys establish hierarchies within their peer groups. Leaders do emerge, and they dictate the type and duration of play. The subordinate boys in the group fall into their tiers enthusiastically and willingly. They seem instinctively to know how to make submissive gestures towards the leaders, although it is possible that they have learned these at home. Subordinate boys work hard to maintain the hierarchy, and will turn on those lower in the hierarchy who attempt to promote another male to a position of dominance.

This is all recognizably male-type play, and similar behaviour can be observed among adult primates. It could be hypothesised that instinctive (and some learned) behaviour in boys is generated by an accumulation of limited experience, immaturity and a developing IQ which puts them temporarily on a par with other primates. Much human juvenile male play is directed towards the establishment and maintenance of superiority over other males.

It is unlikely, however, that pre-adolescent boys fear girls enough to attempt to exert superiority over them. Boys and girls rarely play together, and pair playing with the cautious exploration of sex differences is unlikely to propagate the attitudes that result in the adult male's view of the female.

The lessons don't end at home or in the street. The

99

differences are reinforced at school, especially up to the age of five. In a class of pre-primary school children, it has been noticed that the teachers are more attentive to boys than they are to girls. Furthermore, the help they give to boys is more likely to lead to independence. Girls are taught to be more dependent. Nursery school teachers (women) have been observed to encourage girls to touch each other freely, while boys were discouraged from doing so. Boys were actively encouraged to play 'male' games and girls were steered towards the dolls and the wendy house. And if there was any tendency to cross the gender line, teachers swiftly moved in to put in a stop to such 'aberrant' behaviour.

Are teachers aware that they are doing this? It is sobering to ponder that in these classes the teachers are almost always women. Even in schools where a stated aim was to avoid sex typing, stereotypes were being unconsciously perpetuated. Girls were complimented for wearing pretty dresses but not when they wore pretty trousers. Boys got no compliments for nice clothes. When boys fought, they received praise.

Why should teachers, particularly female ones, unconsciously want to help create the dominant male? Are they merely looking after their jobs? It is just possible that a father who hears that his young son and heir fools around with dolls at kindergarten is going to see to it that someone gets the sack. But the reasons may be far deeper than the fear of losing a job. The teacher may be driven by forces well outside her own control. Her ancestor created man to protect and provide for her, and it is therefore in her own interests to do all she can to help to release into the world as perfect a specimen of the aggressive, independent and dominant male as she can. It matters not that she may have read books pointing out the injustices embedded in a gender-oriented society. Despite the exhortations of friends and newspaper articles she knows, really knows, how the males out there feel about competition from women. Far safer to stick to rules laid down many thousands of years ago. By the same token she will teach little girls the way she herself was taught as a child.

The problem doesn't stop in nursery school. As children grow older they continue to get powerful messages, particularly in mixed sex schools, which reinforce fixed ideas about male dominance and female passivity. It is evident that in the classroom boys get more publicity for bad behaviour. Cause trouble and you're sure to be noticed, not only by the teacher, but also by the rest of the class. Boys will also get punished for violent and aggressive behaviour, the punishment itself often violent and aggressive. Boys notice that girls receive less harsh punishments and conclude that girls must be a weaker sex. Boys also learn early on that rough behaviour gets them into the limelight. They do not fail to notice dad's covert approval when they are punished for fighting.

And it isn't only during social interactions that boys are taught to view themselves as superior to girls. They are encouraged to take academic subjects that have been considered for many years to be 'too difficult' for girls.

One of the more sexually slanted subjects at school is undoubtedly mathematics. Traditionally, boys are encouraged to study maths, which is a subject associated with prestigious and high status jobs. Teachers of maths are more likely to be men. In some schools girls are actively discouraged from studying maths. Yet there is no evidence that boys are better at the subject than are girls. This doesn't stop teachers and parents from encouraging boys to do the subject both at school and afterwards at university, and discouraging girls. It follows from this that teachers of maths are more likely to be men than women, and one is tempted to feel that this is yet another example of the male protection racket. There is little doubt that if teachers encouraged girls to do maths, more girls would, and do well in the subject, as has been happening in Britain. Statistics from the British Department of Education show that girls' performance in GCSE mathematics examinations improved dramatically from 1991 to 1992.

Some educationalists would argue that boys and girls (and men and women) show clear-cut differences in the types of mental skills they have, and that these are not learned, but inherent. They will point to several tests which prove that men have better spatial skills than do women. They are better at map-reading, maze problem solving, and at recognizing specified shapes when these are imbedded in complex designs. But where girls and boys are being given equal attention in the classroom, it turns out that girls are performing as well as, and in some cases better than, the boys in many spheres.

The gospel of male superiority continues to be preached, however, by the media.

Would Batwoman have been as successful a film as was Batman? Why wasn't Tarzan a woman? The answer, quite simply, lies in the box office receipts. They just wouldn't pull in the customers. Any boy who takes his movies seriously has no doubt that you need a Rambo or Schwarzenegger to get things done, and a woman would only get in the way. If she is involved in the action, she's usually in trouble and threatened with death or worse, and, ironically enough, it is only the raging, glistening, muscle-rippling male who can help. His reward is of course her body.

Women make lousy screen heroes for the male viewer. They just aren't believable in the macho theme park of artificial violence. They don't do it in real life so why should they do it on the big screen. A man walks out of the cinema shaken and stirred after a dose of Robert De Niro as *Raging Bull*, and sits hypnotized through Coppola's *Apocalypse Now*. He can even identify with male American Indian heroes in Kostner's film *Dances with Wolves*. But the same guy slouches out of Woody Allen's *Hannah and her*

Sisters feeling vaguely cheated.

Similarly, television advertisements leave us in no doubt as to the natural superiority and importance of the male. He is out there ruling big business, driving superb motor cars or jetting in to a golden beach where a stunning blonde in a transparent pink dress stands barefoot waiting to run (in slow motion) to her man. Her sister might stand flustered before a washing machine while the visiting engineer subliminally seduces her with the potency of his washing powder and his masculinity.

The advertisers know what they're doing. They appreciate the thinness of the veneer. They can peel it away more easily than you can peel a banana. And in a boy or girl that veneer is exceedingly thin. The developing mind is very close to its ancestry. The lines are open and reinforcement of the message is going on all the time.

It is not surprising, therefore, to learn that boys would hate to be girls, and many girls would much rather be boys. American boys who were asked how they would see themselves as girls answered that they would have to spend more time at home helping mother, be more concerned about appearance and worry about being raped. They felt that they would be much more restricted. Girls felt that as boys they would have far more freedom, be liberated from a sex-object status and, poignantly, get more time with their father. In view of this, it is worth trying to find out in more depth how the father, or his absence, affects the home and the child.

There is plenty of evidence that by the second half of an infant's first year, an emotional bond is formed between the infant and one or both of its parents. Between the ages of nine to twenty-four months, infants direct attachment and affiliative responses to parents and strangers. However, babies do not show clear-cut differences in preference for mothers or fathers if both are available. If preferences are shown, it is all from the parental side. In other words, favouritism stems from parents and not from their children.

As far as play is concerned, the influence of the father over his child is far more powerful than that of the mother. Mothers tend to engage in more dainty and conventional games such as pat-a-cake, while fathers like more rough-and-tumble play. By the time an infant reaches its second year, it will initiate physical games with a father, and as the infant gets older, the frequency of physical play increases. In a laboratory test, two-thirds of children aged two and a half preferred to play with their father rather than with their mother. The influence of the father on the developing child cannot be underestimated. He is in a unique position to imprint attitudes in the minds of the children of either sex.

Parents, especially mothers and young first-timers, when alerted to the problem of stereotyping react with some fear and apprehension. What ought they to do? What is best for the child? If the parental behavioural input is so influential in determining gender regardless of sex, how is a parent to behave? Is it better to stand back and allow gender to develop from within the very young child, and to try to counter the peer group pressures that will inevitably come the child's way? Or should one consciously accept the way things are and adopt the pink for girls and blue for boys philosophy?

If nature dictates gender as rigidly as it dictates sex, then attempts to distort the self-image could be very damaging, creating strains within the developing child that would present as neuroses or worse later in life. A parent or parents who deliberately coach their son to believe that non-violent, non-competitive play is good and preferable to violent tumbling and fighting may not be doing him any favours. Those who send a crying son back into the boyhood jungle to turn the other cheek instead of striking back may turn a future success story into one of failure. A mild-mannered, yielding boy with soaring poetic vision is not going to be suitable material for a father with hopes of creating a shipping magnate or heavyweight boxer.

On the other hand, it might be argued that without parental intervention a potentially wonderful, well-focused and gender-normal future adult may never happen because the child was allowed to wander unguided. If the boy was not fondled and tossed often into the air as a baby, if he was not tumbled in play-fights with his dad, and if he was not dissuaded from playing with his mum's bra, stockings and lipstick, is it possible that he might grow up to be unsure of his gender?

No answers to those questions are available. But through observing parents at play in a wide range of cultures, some common patterns emerge. It appears that no matter where in the world one looks, fathers are rougher with sons than they are with daughters. They are not generally brutal or cruel, just rough, and one wonders whether there isn't a genetic component to gender-directed behaviour after all, and that attempting to modify or interfere with it could be damaging to the father as well as the son. Learning and pattern imprinting is a two-way process, and it is possible that by allowing his instincts to govern the nature of his play and other activities with his son, that a father is giving expression to his own masculinity. If fathers consciously suppress this expression, they too may become stressed.

The human father, no less than the lion, wants to nurture and grow more males, to ensure the survival of his genes. He is primarily concerned to protect his own offspring and cares little, if anything, for the genes of another male. Human societies ensure that the male's role development and ultimate self-image are reinforced both inside and outside the home.

By the time a boy gets to being a man he is primed and ready to be one. And at this point he discovers that he is going out of fashion, especially at work.

6
Managing the Male

In December, 1990, Sarah Hogg was appointed Policy Advisor to the Prime Minister John Major. She had taken a first at Oxford, spent around thirteen years working for the Economist, a few years as economics editor for the Sunday Times business news and at Channel 4 as a news presenter before going on to the Times and then to the Independent as economics editor. She has a reputation for brilliance and ruthless efficiency, and it is said that only a fool becomes her enemy. Her advice is valued and there is little doubt that she influences decisions which will dictate the future of the country. If this description had appeared in print fifty years ago, it would have been assumed that a man was being described.

Consider also the ship's complement on HMS Brilliant when she sailed into the Gulf War. Of the 254 sailors on board, twenty were female. And they were sailing into combat. They lived under the same conditions as the men, ate the same food, heard male language and probably used similar if not identical adjectives if the need arose. The Wrens on board ship knew how to do the same jobs as did the men, had received the same training, received the same pay and faced the same dangers. The American Navy, incidentally, refused to expose its women sailors to the dangers of combat. In December, 1991, the British Armed Forces Minister, Archie Hamilton, announced that women would in future be trained to fly jets into combat, both in the Navy and the Army. Women would be given the same rigorous flight training as are men, and would be entrusted with machines costing many millions of pounds. This is quite a turnaround, when one considers that up until 1989 women were not even allowed to fly transport aircraft.

Women have made it to the top. The success of Margaret Thatcher as Britain's first woman prime minister needs no retelling. In November 1990, Mary Robinson was confirmed as Ireland's first woman president. Her success is all the more impressive if one looks at the policies she espouses in a Catholic-dominated country. A practising Catholic herself, she advocates access to contraception, the introduction of divorce, the abolishment of laws which make homosexuality a crime and the promotion of information about abortion. One would expect that in Ireland those views wouldn't get a male politician to first base. But President Robinson made it to the top with those views, and one wonders just how many men would have had the guts to carry them on the way up.

Women are now visible, and in some cases dominant in all spheres of work. They can be found laying bricks, digging tunnels, running hospitals and on the bench in the High Court, when not so long ago they were chaining themselves to the railings of 10 Downing Street in a fight to get the vote. It is a triumph won in the face of great odds, those odds having been created by male attitudes which, in many cases and in many countries, are still the same as they were a thousand years ago. In Britain, the views of men on the suitability of women for certain forms of work are well documented.

It is instructive to consider the view of a Victorian male: 'Whilst recognizing the occasional utility of a man as a nurse we are inclined to think that the occupation is one which is more safely left in the hands of women ... '

These words, written by a Victorian British physician for the lay public, tactfully express male sentiment regarding the role of women in medicine. It is also an example of the blatant hypocrisy of the Victorian 'gentleman' who forbade his wife to work; he did not lay this constraint on working class women, who enjoyed more freedom, it seems, in the sweat shops of the textile industry. Our physician would have been aghast (frightened?) at the thought of a female doctor. He would have been firmly of the opinion that women are not able to do the same jobs as men, that their inferior strength, intellect and lack of emotional control rendered them unfit for the work which was properly the preserve of the male. These deficiencies made it safer (for their own dear sakes) to keep women at home and in the kitchen where they would stay out of trouble. Had the learned physician been aware of the evidence that the male and female brain are wired differently, he would most probably have exclaimed: 'Aha! It is just as I thought.' He would have pointed out what he had read in the anatomy books: that the female brain is smaller than that of the male.

What *are* modern man's preserves? His ancient urge to hunt drives him as hard as it ever did. But today the prairies are wheat fields, the jungles nature reserves. The animals have vanished therefore man has had to find other prey. So he hunts wealth. Not only does he hunt it, he prides himself on his ability to get it. Why, otherwise, should he make the sport his own preserve? It's an illusion that he sallies out every day to provide for his grateful family. On the contrary, he isn't trying to impress them at all. He's out to impress himself and other men. He scales the heights of the bank balance, and when he makes it to the top he is every bit as swollen with achievement as the man who carried home the leg of a reindeer. Even if that primitive spouse probably teamed up with several others to kill the animal, he took home his meat with pride. Possibly they had to fight off a ravenous rival group who lived on the other side of the hill. That would have given the meat yet more spice for him.

He didn't look like a stockbroker, but give him a shave, a bath and a dark suit and you wouldn't give him a second glance in the elevator. He's still with us, and he is every bit the killer he was then. He knows his strengths and he knows what he can and cannot do. He knows he has nothing on the female who performs miracles back home, so he acknowledges defeat on that count and turns his sights on the office, on the building site, on a ship or in an aeroplane, or in the lecture or operating theatre. For thousands of years he marked out his territory, and firmly kept women off his patch. But now they are prowling all over his land; no matter where he looks, there they are, and they are eating his grass and killing his animals. What's worse, they are getting to the kill before he can. So he is raising his weapons and sighting them not only at his prey but at women as well.

Nobody will argue with the statement that men dominate the workplace. In no other sphere of activity have the barriers been more firmly erected and jealously guarded. The statistics do all the talking. In the United States in the early '80s, 98% of all pre-school and kindergarten teachers were women; 99% of nurses; 84% of elementary school teachers; 83% of librarians; 73% of laboratory technicians. All these are badly paid jobs with low status (in the eyes of men). On the other hand, 4.4% of engineers were women; 4.6% of dentists; 14.1% of lawyers and judges; 13.1% of physicians; 38.5% of accountants; 35.3% of college and university teachers. Very similar figures were found for British women for the '70s. And at all levels, men were paid twice as much for the same job. There are no prizes for guessing the sex of more than 95% of all cleaners – women (char*ladies*) of course..

So what, women say, things are changing. Indeed they are, and too fast for the male to cope with. Let's look more closely at the reasons for those figures, and how the changing work scene affects the male.

Those numbers represent the order of things before the Womens' Movement started to make an impact. In other words, they reflect the natural way of working life according to men, and almost certainly to most women until very recently. Similar statistics would have been produced in ancient Sumeria, Babylon, Alexandria, Jerusalem, Greece or Rome. The pattern has been deeply grooved into the male brain over the centuries. One stops short of suggesting that the ability to be an engineer is imprinted on the Y chromosome. Essentially, nothing has changed for thousands of years. From the time that human society settled into an urban lifestyle, men have dominated the workplace and done all the important jobs outside the home. The more dominant men grabbed the interesting and well paid work and channelled the dull, repetitive jobs towards their meeker peers.

But the wives weren't all that dumb. They knew damned well what they were missing. They realised that life is no trial run and they would spend their one and only crack at it up to their armpits in dirty water. They saw what an interesting world men were shaping out there and they itched to get at the action. They knew that men were unlikely to grumble if a woman served them with wine and grilled carp at the local watering hole. After all, their wives did it at home all the time. And so women infiltrated the service industries, such as catering, cooking, cleaning, hairdressing and so on. But even so, they treaded warily. In their chosen work, women were careful not to aspire to management. That was reserved for men. Even today, three-quarters of these industries are manned (pun unintended) by women, but women occupy less than 5% of the management posts.

Those far-off women were doing the best they could in a society dominated by savage, confident men. They were creating for themselves a niche in the workplace that endures to this day. They took low wages, they convinced their male bosses that they had no aspirations, and they proved it by going off to have babies and working part-time for even less money. In order to placate husbands who saw their wives and daughters going out to work, they convinced them that they, the women, were no good at anything men did so well. They convinced men that women had neither the brains, strength nor the temperament to do a man's job. Men would have been only too ready to accept that neither could nor would a woman venture into the exchange, the bank, the medical school or the coal mine. Men, who hadn't given the feminine psyche a second thought, were given a blueprint of the female mind and they believed it.

Women continued to do the same jobs, the work that required little thought and imagination, the work that led nowhere, the work they had convinced men was beneath them. Men regarded women as inferior in intellect. Why else would women sit for hours on a stool sewing, or serving at table? And as time passed new jobs arose for women and they took those jobs. They became nannies, childminders, nurses (in their millions). Florence Nightingale had convinced men that women were so warm, tender and caring that they were ideal for the purpose. And why not, reasoned the men; what self-respecting male wants to change a bedpan?

And so the years witnessed the silent, patient march of millions of women into the nursery schools, into the sewing mills and into the yards where they scraped the scales off millions of fish. Women manned the telephone exchanges and the typewriters and gritted their teeth but remained silent when men at work stroked their backsides and slid their hands down their dresses to cup their breasts.

Of course women did have power, but it was unofficial. Some could and did extend the arm of influence into society indirectly through their husbands. These women knew the axiom that you can have power without influence and influence without power, and in the home they had the latter and they used it. Their men, as often as not, never realised how much their decisions and actions were dictated by their wives. The impact these wives and mistresses had on the course of the Womens' Movement should not be underestimated.

Enter the twentieth century. The male mind exploded into realms of nature and scientific discovery that now promise to lay bare the unthinkable secrets of creation. And women couldn't stand it any longer, not in western societies anyway. So they broke out of the home and bearded the lion. They forced him to give them the vote. They muttered about accountancy, high-powered branches of medicine and engineering. Other women watched breathlessly. This was heady stuff and dangerous as hell. Didn't these daring women realise that by leaving home they were also leaving a space that could be filled by another woman? And what would the men do? Stunningly, the male gave way, albeit with sour grace, this male who has been known to strangle his daughter if she so much as looked at a man.

So what was the difference?

It was, simply, that the male didn't believe, deep down where the genes are, that he was any better than women. He knew that for the first time he was coming under real threat, where it hurt most, in his own hunting grounds. He didn't believe for a moment that women would fall by the way, overcome with inadequacy. On the contrary, he feared these animals who wielded so much power over him at home. If they could manage such miracles as menstruation and childbirth, what could they not achieve in a bank or operating theatre?

While it was slowly dawning on the male that the good times were coming to an end, women began to realise what they were up against. They began to appreciate the flip side of the coin their female ancestors had tossed. For those women long ago had gambled on being able one day to take on the men without knowing the nature of the ultimate battle.

Modern women accepted the challenge. They looked at several possibilities. They asked themselves some questions. Are we really inferior mentally? Are we really unfitted for managerial and professional work? Is there a biological difference between the male and the female human brain? These are brave questions to ask. After all, what happens if you get an unequivocal 'yes' to any one of them?

Men have ready answers to these questions. They have known about women all along. I quote: 'A woman's intellect is normally more feeble and her curiosity greater than those of a man; furthermore it is undesirable to set her to studies that may turn her head.'

Those words were written by a seventeenth-century French Archbishop, one Fénelon. He had no grounds for believing what he wrote. Women had never proven to him that what he propounded was true. They had never been given a chance to do so. He simply echoed what men thought they knew about women, *what women had taught them to believe.*

In 1903 Havelock Ellis, a psychologist, suggested that the male population has a wider range of mental ability, implying that women can never run alongside the male high-fliers. In 1925 another academic, L. Terman, reported after studying 1000 gifted children that there were more boys than girls at the top end of the intelligence range. He didn't realize, however, that he had been fed a biased group by the teachers. But it all fitted in nicely. And since then, millions of numbers have been crunched in an attempt to confirm it. And they say loud and clear that there are no differences between male and female intellect. The only cranial exercise men do better than women is a test of spatial ability mentioned in Chapter 5.

The twentieth century is the century of numbers. Numbers crawl over our lives like ants over a hill of honey, and now they are being used to prove or disprove the conception man has of the working woman. Not only are women counting the women at work, but they are also counting opinions about them in the hope that they can come up with the Truth About Women and Work. And, not surprisingly, in the light of the above, women are finding that there is nothing men do in the workplace that they can't do as well. The only thing holding them back was, and is, their poor self-image which they took on board so long ago. There was a lot of re-evaluating to do.

What was needed was a complete turnaround. And the fuel to drive this mental gymnastic was the realisation that it is the job that affects the person, not the person who affects the job. If women accepted the premise that they were intellectually the equal of men then they could learn a lot about themselves by observing men who were observing men at work, especially in jobs offering what women didn't have, i.e. opportunities for advancement. Women also did studies of their own. The results are very interesting.

Essentially, men whose advancement is blocked start behaving according to the female working stereotype – the worker in a dead-end job. They lose interest in their superiors, in fact they ignore them altogether and become socially involved at work with colleagues or men in inferior positions. Women in blue collar jobs do exactly the same. Men who are kept down are noisier, more talkative, or sullen and withdrawn. They threaten to leave, take time off and concentrate on hobbies and home life.

If, however, a blue collar worker (man or woman) doing a routine, repetitive job with no prospect is given the opportunity for advancement he or she will suddenly develop a keen, creative interest in the work. Social life is relegated to third place and a lively curiosity about powerful supervisors and managers substituted. In short, ambition replaces apathy.

Armed with this knowledge, one would think women could slip easily into the management structure. Not so. For this is the male's ultimate preserve, his last hunting ground. In order to break in, women needed to tread with care. This was new, dangerous territory, and their hold was extremely tenuous.

Management hits at the heart of the matter. The occupation is immaterial. Management is universal; it comes into all work. It's the difference between power and submission. Managers rule. When men talk about management they bring in the adjectives of gender. Managers are described as forceful, aggressive, decisive, logical, enterprising, ambitious. It doesn't sound like a woman at all who is labelled weak, tender, warm, weepy, noisy, giggly, illogical, impulsive – in short, poor management material. The stereotypes even persuade women. Many women if asked will affirm that they are fitted for 'women's jobs' only, and that excludes management. Job interviewers, whether they be men or women, have those adjectives embedded in their brains, and when a woman walks through the door, guess which adjectives leap to mind?

Those women who have made it to the managerial chair have done so at a cost. On the way they have had to betray womanhood. They had to fool men into thinking that even in his hunting grounds they were no threat after all. There was only one way to do this, and that was by becoming a token.

Once she was ensconced in her position, a woman set about making herself acceptable to her male colleagues. She had been appointed as a token, that is as a sop to the equal opportunities ethic. She knew she was a discordant note in the all-male managerial structure and had to convert this to one which was more harmonious. She was under constant scrutiny and far too conspicuous for her unique properties rather than for those which she shared with the group. Furthermore, she was under pressure to behave like a female stereotype. Men expected a mother, a pet (baby sister), or sex object. She could have slipped into the shadows by giving men the credit for her success. But that would have resulted in a weakening of her work performance. Instead she did the job that she was paid for and was promptly labelled the iron maiden by her resentful and terrified male colleagues. There wasn't much that they could do about it, however, since bosses seldom fire good managers. But she had put herself on a high, lonely hill. To lessen the isolation, she had to knife other women. This is where betrayal came into it. She joined the men in limiting the numbers of new women managers. In the first place, she didn't need the competition, and also she did not want the men to feel their organization was about to be swamped by hordes of aggressive, power-hungry women. Thus it is not surprising that today in Britain women hold 2% of all board seats.

Nowadays we know that the barriers in western society are crumbling fast. Through their own lobbying, women have seen to it that legislation protects them from exploitation at work, and gives them the right to enter every male preserve.

Even the Church of England, whose Synod in the past all but shed blood to try to prevent the ordination of women bishops, has conceded defeat. And it was a resounding defeat for many of its male members. The Church has always held the view that God decreed that women were the most dangerous creatures on earth. After all, if not for Eve...

On Tuesday, 11 November, 1992, the Synod voted by a majority of five votes to ordain women priests, thereby overturning 2000 years of male domination in the Church. Women exploded with joy. The Archbishop of Canterbury called for calm, and a group of male priests grimly proclaimed their intention to create a schism. One thousand priests will quit the Church, declared the Archdeacon of Leicester. Pity if they do, commented a female lay preacher; but, she added, there are a thousand women waiting to take their place. And they will too.

It is interesting that the arguments put forward by the men who spoke against women priests are very similar to those delivered by the men who fought to retain slavery: the concept of slavery was natural; it was sanctioned by the Bible, and furthermore this wasn't the time to abolish slavery.

One by one the walls come tumbling down.

If women build statues and create heroes and saints, they should make their tallest monument to the countless 'ordinary' women throughout history who laid their bodies one upon another to make stepping stones to freedom for their sisters of the future.

The diehard male may still say, this is all very well, but man, by nature of his hunting instincts, will always have the top jobs. But when one looks at the different types of male in the world today a pattern emerges. Not every male is a born success. Some will never make it to the top; they won't even get half-way up the ladder, even if it's all they think about. Success will elude many men.

Success at work is very important to the male: from the moment he starts work till the day he dies he will be preoccupied with success or the lack of it. The drive to succeed is so deeply imprinted on the male psyche that it is virtually a biological need. If he does not achieve success, his failure will be apparent in his posture, dress, mannerisms, speech and attitudes to others.

Success means different things to different men. It may be the attainment of wealth, fame, power, women or intellectual status or the whole bang shoot. But whatever the aim, the unifying principle is the need to associate himself with and be recognized by other successful men, and to distance himself from failure and those who fail.

The successful man is relatively easy to identify. He usually stands and sits up straight. He cares for his appearance and hygiene, and his personal habits are impeccable. He approaches other men confidently and makes direct, relaxed eye contact. When speaking, his eyes don't slide away when he wants to contradict or express an opinion. When two men are talking, he is likely to break into their conversation and dominate it. Physically, height is immaterial. Many short men are successful, and their voices are often deeper and more penetrating than those of other short men.

A successful man is generally born, not made. He is intelligent, shrewd and selfish, a quality he keeps well hidden on the way up. He probably has an IQ of 125 or higher, and was brought up by confident parents who provided good role models for hard work and careful decision-making. His qualities appear early on, and an astute teacher can point out life's future winners very quickly. By the time he finishes secondary education he is mature enough to understand and manipulate other men. He has gravitas. He is quiet at work while his more boisterous colleagues whoop and joke themselves into obscurity, and he resists the impulse to make a pass at a woman he finds attractive. He is not one of the touchers, feelers and squeezers. When he speaks to women at work he maintains eye contact and never allows his eyes to fall to their breasts or knees. Any sexual liaisons he does have are kept well away from work.

The successful man does not rush into decisions, and delays those he does not need to take immediately. If an unpopular decision needs to be taken, he will delegate it to someone he does not like. But when he does take a decision he sees that it is the right one and that he gets the credit for it. Basically, he is not so preoccupied with his own image that the world is shut out. He wants to know what others are thinking about and does not hesitate to ask them their opinions. He listens hard to what he is being told, and summarizes it in his diary afterwards.

He has an iron rein on his personality. He never loses his temper and he never raises his voice. He breezes carefully through the day and nothing seems to get him down. He seems to resent no one their successes, and in fact is usually the first to congratulate others. He is careful never to speak against a colleague, and remains silent when others do so. He knows that whatever is said against another person gets back very fast. He never forgets to write a thank-you letter, and keeps in touch with people even after they have left the firm. He is well organized and has everything systematically filed.

But most importantly, he works like hell. He doesn't only work for himself, however. He sizes up his colleagues, and he makes sure he does work for those whom he feels will be useful to him. He never turns down a request for help, no matter who asks. He has a reputation for being the one to ask if you want to know anything. He almost always knows the answer. If he doesn't, he'll have it within the hour. If the boss's son or daughter comes into the office to work part-time during the school holidays he will see to it that they have a good time. And when he is invited to a dinner he never arrives empty-handed. Similarly, when he entertains, he leaves out virtually no one immediately connected with his work. He places his feet carefully on the tightrope. Naturally this involves a lot of thought and hard work. But it pays off in spades.

He would never be able to do all this unless he was able to appreciate where he stood in relation to other people. And most men don't, and will never do so. He sounds like the boss's answer to a prayer. He is what virtually every man at work could be if he were able to break out of his personality prison. In other words, he performs at work just like a woman. It's no wonder, then, that the invasion of the workplace by women poses such a threat to most men.

The potential failure shows his colours early in life. At school he is generally a misfit, poor at most subjects except the odd one or two for which he has a genuine flair. He may be withdrawn or the class clown. Teachers and other children instinctively dislike him. Many teachers recognize their own failure in his. He probably has poor role models at home, where he is intensely unhappy. He cannot conceive of himself as a success and he will fulfil his own poor expectations of himself. He has a huge well of self-destructiveness which he shares with many other males.

As he grows older, he will be presented with opportunities, and instead of taking the simple, direct route to success, he will allow his personality to intrude and will confuse, anger and frustrate those who try to help him. He has surrounded himself by such a dense personality fog that he cannot see out of it. He is blind to what other people are or want. He plunges through the day in search of his own wants and needs, and in the process leaves scores of flattened toes in his wake. He does favours for no one because it just doesn't occur to him. He is often boisterous, noisy and lecherous. He fondles the women, and often breezes out of his office in search of sexual titillation. If he is married his colleagues watch contemptuously. Gradually he realizes he isn't getting anywhere and he starts resenting those who are on the way up. He makes offensive remarks, seeming not to care who hears, and his moods blacken. He may spend hours at work dozing and he takes days off.

He has to find signs of success somewhere and he turns to his own body. He can still do some things properly. He masturbates frequently and becomes preoccupied with basic functions such as defecation. He may even regard a loud fart as an achievement. He is moving inexorably towards his personal nemesis. His self-destructive urges intensify until he resolves the problem by breaking down.

Women are proving to be superb competitors for male jobs. They are vocal in their criticism of failure, and since most jobs are still done by men it is inevitable that many men are being criticised by women for incompetence at work. This will serve to heighten the tension.

Now that the recession is here the presence of women in the labour market is a wild card with incalculable consequences. There aren't enough jobs for men any-more, let alone the vast army of hopeful women who are leaving schools, colleges and universities in their thou-sands to seek work. Inevitably, they will displace and bar men from jobs, and tensions are bound to rise.

On the face of it a problem has been solved for many women, that of sexual equality at work. But every scientist knows that solutions create new problems. And this particular problem concerns the male. He is being pushed gently but firmly out of his hunting ground into a country barren of game. He is being told he should enter the realm of women's work, take on the duties which she abandoned in favour of outside work. He should go into the home and assume the duties of the woman. He may have to do it. He may don the apron and tend the baby and the washing machine, but the part of him that is male will rebel and take its toll. Deprived of a quarry, his male hormone testosterone, will wane. His threshold to stress will become lower. He will become unstable and unpredictable. His resentment against his usurper will grow. He will either subside into a condition of pseudo female or third sex, or he will strike out at the only prey left to him, women, who did this to him in the first place.

7

Crawling Under the Pipe Stem

The duties of a wife among the Bantu of the North Kavirondo in East Africa as described in 1949 are explicitly defined. She must sweep, grind, cook, build the fires and clean out the cattle partition. She has to carry water from the spring, buy cooking pots, gather firewood and fetch the salt, i.e. burn salt reeds in special pits and filter the ashes. She must clean the walls of the house and the surface of the yard with cow-dung, beat the floor of the house so that it becomes level and hard and she must hoe the garden. She must also know about the food on the food shelf.

The husband too has duties. He must take care of his sitting stool and beer pipe. He has to watch the cattle, goats and sheep and choose where his wife will dig a garden by first cutting the grass there. He must know when the roof needs mending, pull grass for the mending and plait the string with which the thatcher will tie the grass.

The husband possesses the front of the house; that is 'the husband's side'. The rear, including the cooking stones, side door and yard constitute the 'wife's side'. He has the privilege of owning and sitting on a stool. She must sit on the ground. When he has male friends in to drink beer, the men sit in a circle round a beer pot and suck beer through long reed pipes. If the wife wishes to pass them she must crawl on her belly under the reeds while the men are allowed to step freely over them.

He expects and gets complete obedience from his wife. He is polygamous and can seek another wife if he can afford it. He owns exclusive sexual rights over her. If he turns out to be impotent, his brother will step into his place to try to fertilize her. If she is unfortunate enough to bear only female offspring this is entirely her fault. She is completely dependent on him and she is allowed to own nothing.

This clear sexual dimorphism of roles is not confined to the tribes of the Kavirondo. Throughout tribal Africa, virtually without exception, the duties of husband and wives in their traditional homelands and tribal societies are strictly and immutably proscribed. The man is a hunter and herder. He looks after livestock, protects them from thieves and predators, and deals with barter. He does all the transactions on behalf of the nuclear family unit. Women are not simply discouraged from these duties; they are forbidden to take part. Furthermore, women would not even consider attempting to cross the line of demarcation. This universal sexual difference in domestic function is no accident. It is unlikely that it evolved independently in isolated tribal societies. It is more probable that the pattern was established and radiated, probably from the heart of Africa to the rest of the continent, and from there to the world as man migrated and took his ancestral customs with him. Support for this hypothesis can be obtained simply by turning one's gaze to the world outside Africa.

Strict Islamic law demands that women be segregated from the public lives of men by the practice of purdah, a Persian word meaning curtain. Women in purdah keep their faces covered in public, even before their husbands. They are rarely seen by male visitors to the home and may be required to use a back entrance. A woman who dares to be seen unveiled in a public place is considered to be a wanton and worthy of contempt. Indeed, in some cultures she is putting her life at risk. A young girl who allows her glance to linger a little too long on a young man might well be put to death by her father. An Arab man who kills his wife or daughter for what he considers improper behaviour will receive a sympathetic hearing from his peers.

How did these male attitudes arise? We don't know, but it is certain that they were established a long time ago since they are so widespread. What social imperative, then, forced him to adopt a single female as his mate and to set up home with her? This is a good question, since it addresses not only the problem of the origin of marriage, but also the factors that kept him above the pipe stem and her below. There can be little doubt that those inequalities were a consequence of the prolonged male-female relationship. It may be instructive to go back to the motives of the proto-male of Chapter 1 for a while.

He was concerned about only one thing reproductively, and that was to spread his genes and thus conserve them. Whether he was aware of that is immaterial at this stage. So is his species. As he grew smarter with the passage of much time, by which he was now a fully fledged male as we know him, he realized that casual sex with a passing female was no guarantee that his genes were secure for another generation. There were plenty of other males in the neighbourhood, and any one of those might have been invited to copulate with (or forced himself upon) the female he had just left. Since copulation might be a matter of seconds, it could literally happen if he turned his back on her. It was much easier to cuckold a male than a female, and he could well end up looking after another male's young. It made sense, therefore, to stay around and guard the female and thus his own genes. And if he kept her well stocked with food while she gestated his young, so much the better.

It was not in the male's nature to hang around once he had fertilized the female. He had itchy feet and wanted the excitement of a new territory, another female. But he had to suppress the urge to roam, and keep other males away until he was sure his own progeny were ready to leave the nest, hole, cave, set or hut. And if we look at other species, we find many examples of males who appear to be fanatical about keeping other males away from their mates.

The North American bison weighs about 1000 kg, twice the weight of the female. For about three weeks of the year the males rut and the females go into oestrus – they are receptive. The bulls who win their fights are usually the ones who copulate. A male will pair up with a female and 'tend' her. After copulation he tends her jealously for around half an hour and then he abandons her. This is because he knows that from now on she will refuse to allow any other male to mount her. So their 'marriage' lasts thirty minutes or so, and the male leaves, satisfied that his sperm, and only his, have been introduced into the female. He has successfully effected his anti-cuckoldry manoeuvre. He then goes on to a brief union with another female. Notice the important sex difference here, and also how inexorably the female is imprisoned within her own sex. Not for her the pleasure of another carnal meeting. Unlike the male, who is free to copulate with several more cows, she has had her lot for the season.

Life isn't always this simple for the male. The male starling, for example, guards his mate fanatically during the egg-laying period, to the extent of leaving the nest unguarded when she moves away from it. Other starlings then drop their own eggs into it and he ends up nurturing another male's genes. He has in effect been cuckolded.

Is the female also concerned to protect a carefully chosen insemination, and is she driven by the same pressures as is the male? The evidence is confusing. There is no doubt that in many species she goes to a lot of trouble to pick the best of the bunch. But consider the female baboon, who is nearer to us, in evolutionary terms, than are birds. Once she has taken a mate she will nevertheless move up to and copulate with several males of another troop. This is feminine promiscuity. She has no idea which of her partners will be the parent if there are offspring from her multiple unions. She does not seem to share the male's preoccupation with the fate of the sperm he has introduced into her.

At least one partnership lasts forever. Swans form permanent pair-bonds, and if one partner is killed the other will pine to death.

Returning to the proto-male once more, it is possible to conclude that the male was torn between two strategies: to stay with the female to care for one or more young, or to take the route of promiscuity. Doubtless those two ancient mutual exclusives cemented themselves into his genes and have warred there ever since.

Here, then, was the origin of the pair-bond, the anti-cuckoldry drive and, as it evolved in humans, marriage.

Marriage is a peculiarly human institution. And it's practised in one form or another in every society on earth. It is universally characterized by a commitment to rearing young, sexual access to the female and what we call being faithful. It is, on the face of it, a reproductive union. But marriage means a lot more than that to the male. It is an anti-cuckoldry device; a contract between men which is supposed to guarantee a husband exclusive sexual access to his wife or wives, thus allowing him to be certain that his genetic input is not in vain. It also represents an opportunity to express his ambitions, to demonstrate his material wealth and to proclaim his masculine dominance. In some societies he does this by taking as many females as he can. That is the practice of polygamy, which probably began with the advent of agriculture which allowed men to accumulate wealth. There is little, if any, polygamy among hunter-gatherers such as the Bushmen of the Kalahari. Australian Aboriginals, however, do practise it, but in a very relaxed fashion, and co-wives frequently indulge in adultery with young males of the tribe who are unattached.

Polygamy is much rarer than monogamy. Women do, after all, have minds of their own. It is all the more puzzling, therefore, that they allow themselves to be herded together for the sole use of one man. It also puts a strain on society when many women are withheld from the male population, many of whom are forced into celibacy. Nevertheless, some men have been able to build up huge harems, containing upwards of 100 women; all that was needed was money and a strong physical constitution. It is most unlikely that any one man could form a significant emotional attachment with more than a very few of his 'wives'. This was not an important consideration to him. Possibly his most pressing need to was to keep the peace.

There is no doubt that the monogamous marriage is an artificial arrangement where the male is concerned. He just wasn't designed for it. He finds the sexual commitment to one woman a strain. From the proto-male down to the present human, there is little attempt to limit promiscuity. Literature thrives on the eternal struggle in the male breast between carnal desire and noble fidelity. In real life it isn't hard to predict which way he'll go if given a safe opportunity. In one study of American and German men, over 40% interviewed expressed a willingness to indulge in casual sex, as opposed to 5% of women, and one wonders just how honest the other 60% of men were. In Israel, where children are brought up in coeducational dormitories, around half the boys and less than 10% of girls interviewed in one study thought that casual sex was acceptable. The Wellcome Trust recently supported an in-depth survey of sexual attitudes and practices in Britain which shows that women are less likely to have more than one sexual partner within five years of their child's birth than are the fathers. Clearly, there seems to be a sex difference here.

Marriage is a sacrifice, one which the male will never come to terms with. He has voluntarily given up the opportunity to copulate with women to whom he is attracted. This hits home only after he has slipped the ring onto her finger. He realizes what he has done and wonders how to get out of the mess he has put himself into. If he is confident, aggressive and successful he may continue to seek and copulate with other women. If he dares not break the social taboo, he will fantasize.

The male's view of his wife is exemplified by the Kavirondo couple described at the beginning of this chapter. Her role is not only that of reproductive machine, but also of subservient partner in running a home. A married woman must show other men that she is married, hence the engagement and wedding ring. Men may wear a wedding ring, but society does not place any pressure on them to do so. It is the woman's hand that receives the ring in a church or registry office. And from the moment she puts on the ring and signs the form, she is expected to honour that contract to the letter.

In many societies she is bound by legal contract 'to honour and obey' and the constraints don't end there. Men have formulated laws to protect themselves from cuckoldry. A wife can be punished for adultery. A married woman who has sex with a man other than her husband is guilty of an offence and her husband is considered by other men to be a victim of her adultery. In several ancient civilizations and some modern ones, both the wife and her lover would be put to death. If the husband took it upon himself to take their lives he would almost invariably find plenty of compassion from his peers. Jealous rage and its bloody expression are understood by all men who deal out sympathy and lenient judgement. In Britain, many a charge of murder has been reduced to one of manslaughter. In France the crime of passion is known to be followed by an acquittal. It is a most unusual society in which a woman is given similar recourse against an errant spouse. There are a very small number of cases, however, where married women have received some protection through the courts. The Romans, for example, formulated a law in BC 16, whereby a man, who could normally confiscate his unfaithful wife's dowry, was forbidden to do so if he too was an adulterer. In Austria, in 1852, the first sex equality laws were passed between man and wife. Nevertheless, Austrian (male) lawmakers continued to regard the male cuckold as a victim. A victim he may be, but he can be lethal with it. So, however, can she.

Jealous rage is not the sole preserve of men. Women attack and kill their unfaithful men. This happens relatively rarely, however, and they usually receive short shrift from the courts. Possibly the most celebrated case is that of the English woman, Ruth Ellis, the last woman hanged in Britain before the abolition of the death penalty.

What makes people so angry about infidelity?

Jealousy may be defined as a condition of mind generated by a threat to ownership. Notice that it is not one's love or passion that is cheated, but one's sense of possession, both for men and women. The male owns the woman. Her infidelity is a cuckolding for him. His infidelity cheats her of an important resource, namely his care and protection of her and her children. But it is more than that, or Ruth Ellis would not have killed her faithless lover. She felt that she owned him physically, and that he broke a taboo by sleeping with other women. The concept of ownership, however, stands. It is curious that a man (or woman) is unlikely to kill over a stolen car or watch. A husband will not butcher his wife if she spends his hard-earned cash at the races; she will not react violently if he pawns her jewellery, unless it's to pay for another woman. In America sexual jealousy is virtually the only motive for spouse murder.

Clearly there are different types of possession, and possession of another human being is a very fundamental property of relationships between men and women. In fact, any woman who lives under the same roof as a man, be she lodger or daughter, will sooner or later arouse in him the sense that in some indefinable way he 'owns' her. And he will express this by trying, with varying degrees of subtlety, to constrain her movements. If she is his daughter, he will use force.

In Trinidad, daughters are jealously guarded and their movements may be restricted, the severity of restriction depending on the father's attitude. Apparently, young girls thus guarded tend to be more likely to form a stable relationship with prosperous males in the community. A Lebanese father strangles a daughter who looks at a young man and a Saudi princess is put to death for having sexual intercourse. In societies where the roles of men and women, especially in marriage, are clearly and rigidly defined, the women are tightly controlled. They are confined indoors for much of their lives, and in public are forced to cover themselves from head to toe, a practice called claustration. This has a practical purpose: a woman of reproductive age must be kept marketable. It is the job of the family, and particularly of the women, to guard her against the male. Her virginity is all-important, and in some cultures the husband-to-be or one of his family will inspect her before taking her to wife.

There are at least twenty countries in Africa, Arabia, Indonesia and Malaysia where infibulation is still practised. This is the custom of sewing up a young girl's labia majora only leaving a very small orifice. The smaller the hole, the greater the brideprice. Sexual intercourse is impossible for her. The labia will be cut to allow intercourse with her husband and for delivery. Before going away for any length of time, her husband will have her re-infibulated. Many wives demand re-infibulation to narrow the orifice in order to give their husbands more pleasure. Their anxiety is that he will lose interest in his wife and divorce her and so she will lose everything.

Clearly the human male regards his mate as more than a mere servant; yet in many cultures he has subjugated her mercilessly. This is the great puzzle. If she is so precious to him, and worth dying for, why the cruelty?

In order to answer this question it's necessary to assume that he doesn't think he's being cruel. He is simply exercising his absolute right over a possession hard and expensively won. It is also important to realize that a mate is not like any other possession. She is an extension of the man, an extension fused to him as tightly as his own limbs. And like his limbs, independence from him is not only unacceptable but incomprehensible. It is almost impossible for him to perceive her as human on a par with him.

Thus he never asks her opinion. Would he ask his arm what shares he should buy? Would he consult his liver before choosing a new car? Many a woman will confirm that her husband flies into an unreasonable frenzy of rage if she appears to be taking the decision-making out of his hands, even by just wanting to drive the car for a change. Many a man feels most uncomfortable to be seen by other men in the passenger seat with a woman at the wheel. He squirms, knowing that other men are watching him, waiting to pounce, waiting for signs of weakness in order to take what is his, including his mate. It is like that for a male; he sees other men *taking* her from him.

Man's attitude to his mate is not only shaped by her attractiveness as a possession, even though this is very important. If a man, especially one who is not successful generally with women, is out in public with a strikingly attractive woman, and other men can see him, his facial expression will give him away. Many men cannot fight off a triumphant grin, although the meeker man will temper it with a touch of sheepishness as an act of submission to other men, since he has to some extent shown a form of aggression.

But it is not as simple as all that. The male doesn't regard his mate just as a high-grade servant or a prized trophy. She is his declaration to the world that he is functioning as a successful male, and very little counts for more than this. Her ability to bear offspring, especially male offspring, is thus crucial. It also hits the male hard if his wife leaves him. It is a sign to the world that he does not satisfy her. He may take strong measures to get her back. Doubtless many British women were chilled to read in the Times on 28 November, 1992, that *in Britain* runaway Asian wives are hunted down by paid bounty hunters.

The situation is complicated when the male discovers about the physical functioning of the female, about what happens when he gets close to her on a daily basis, and its possible effects on him. Basically, that closeness inspires terror. Women appear to have magical powers, and one of these magicians is living right under his roof!

The most potent symbol of a man's power and virility is his erect penis. Consider, then, what happens when he inserts it into the female. In the first place he loses his reason while it's inside her. Then she sucks his vital sap out of him, and after he removes his penis from her body it is limp and useless for sex. She then goes on to do something quite awesome: she creates a new human being. Clearly women are potentially dangerous. Not only do they turn a man insane and weaken him, but they have the god-like power of creation. Here is sufficient reason to keep them under firm control lest they use their powers to subjugate men completely. Men have tried to minimize the female's creativity in many widely scattered cultures throughout history, arguing that the male sperm contains the complete new human being in miniature form, and all the female does is to keep it wet and warm.

Envy is the inseparable companion of fear. If men are scared of the powers of women, perhaps they also desire those powers. When a human male bleeds he knows he is in trouble, especially if the blood pours out of a natural orifice. Yet women are able to survive regular floods of blood, year in and year out. The male has tried to show that he too can do this. Why else would the men of some primitive tribes try to give themselves a vulva by slitting the underside of the penis along its length and periodically opening the wound to allow it to bleed in an attempt to imitate menstruation?

Childbirth, too, has always fascinated and frightened the human male. In some cultures, for example among the Arapesh in New Guinea, the father throws himself into his mate's childbirth to the extent of taking to his cot and writhing in agony. This is the practice of 'couvade'. Even after the mother has given birth and returned to work he continues to make a noisy fuss, manifestly designed to draw attention to himself. But more than this, he is making claim to the baby in an attempt to minimize the contribution of the mother. In modern (and not so modern) cultures couvade is not the only means employed to minimize the power of the female. Couvade is more likely to be practised in societies where the males are not strongly organized, and where ritual is the only weapon they possess (apart from force). In societies where the males have got their act together, they can restrict the movements of the female, and remind her that the child she bears is not her property. Thus the baby, especially a son, may be removed from the natural mother after weaning, as Japanese men did with their illegitimate male offspring.

The feeling that the baby and even the mother are the male's 'property' is reinforced if he has had to pay for his wife in the first place. Payment may be formalized, as with the African *lobola*, which the aspirant husband pays the bride's father. This payment may represent a considerable shakedown, and seriously deplete the young man or his father financially, especially if the girl's father is a dab hand at bargaining. Therefore it is not surprising that he feels that she and all the fruits of her labour are his property. If, as may happen, she turns out to be infertile, he has recourse to tribal law, and may demand the services of one of her sisters or cousins. If she doesn't have any, the girl's father might well find he has his merchandise back on his hands at the cost of a full refund, unless she has been maltreated by the husband. Among the Kipsigis of Kenya, for example, a wife may desert her husband and return home, and if it is established that she had good cause, the groom doesn't get back any money. It is therefore surprising that a 'pregnancy' trial isn't a common practice. It seems that male pride overcomes male parsimony virtually every time. Perish the thought of second-hand merchandise. The term isn't used lightly. Two men, fathers both, entered into a contract and a sale was made on the understanding that the goods were sound. No less an authority than Claude Lévi-Strauss defined marriage as a contract between men, although he proposed it as a universal concept, which is debatable. Nevertheless, there are grounds for thinking that modern western fathers also consider that their daughters belong to them, and that they are giving them away in marriage. The practice of the dowry is at odds with this idea. The bride brings the dowry to the marriage.

Despite claiming ownership of women, man feared their powers of creation. He incorporated this fear into his legends. The first gods were women. Men (presumably) fashioned objects such as the Venus of Laussal in France at least 50,000 years ago. The female gods were extravagantly fecund and all powerful. Not only that, they liked and were given human blood. Mother earth was a goddess who gave birth to new life for which she needed a constant supply of young blood.

In the light of all this, it is easier to see why the male is 'cruel' to his female(s).

1. She is a possession, for which he has paid much. His possessions don't dictate to him. More than his other possessions, she is an extension of himself, under his control, and seen by other men to be so. He has never thought of her as an individual with the abilities of a man. Such thoughts are worse than heresy. They are unnatural. He fears the ridicule he will generate if he cannot control his wife. What man wants to be labelled as hen-pecked? In fact a man may kill a wife he feels has given him this image in the eyes of other men.

2. She is a symbol to other men that he is reproductively successful, and she is the exclusive generator of his own genes. If she can't do that she is useless to him and is readily discarded.

3. She is a medal awarded for being more successful than other men, a badge to be flaunted in public. She is displayed in order to enhance the male's image. To be seen to have lost her to another man would be unbearable.

4. She is dangerous because she is big, thinking and capable of independent movement, and must be controlled. Therefore her actions and her domains in the home and outside it are clearly defined.

5. She is capable of weakening him, and literature has warned him about this problem, from the Bible downwards.

6. She is capable of doing much that he can't, especially producing another human being.

She is a far cry from the seductive creature whom he craved before she became his. She is to be hidden, shown off, guarded and controlled. She is, basically, a managerial headache. Man has always been torn between locking her away and flaunting her.

The modern western male may not be as overt as his

Kavirondo counterpart in expressing his attitude towards his mate, but it is there nevertheless. In the home she has her domain, most notably the kitchen, which is tucked well away from the front of the house, apartment, villa or castle. It is her job to see to it that the house is kept clean and the family fed. Their children are to be reared by her, from the initial suckling till they leave school. He expects his wife to maintain her own domains and functions in the home, and feels instinctively wrong about moving into them.

He does not expect her to go out and find the food. Men have been driven to suicide because their wives have had to go out and find work. Do men not say they would rather cut off their *right arm* than allow their wives to go out and work? How many women have seen their husbands slide into psychosis because their wives have to support them? One wonders how the Kavirondo man would react.

The Kavirondo man does not perceive himself as cruel. He sees himself as effective, and he would be puzzled at the charge of physical or mental cruelty. How can he be cruel by controlling what (not whom) he won? What he won he keeps, and if the prize happens to be a creature that functions as a physically independent entity, that creature must be properly managed or it will attack him or escape. The lion tamer knows the problem. He does not underestimate the danger of his animals. But because the creature thinks, albeit in an inferior way, it is more to be feared.

This fear appears to manifest itself just as powerfully outside the home, especially in cases where the male has to make official decisions about the female.

8

The Male in Court

The courts provide a unique opportunity to study the attitudes of the human male towards the female; unique because he has actually had to define and formalize. Since the laws, until relatively recently, have been made almost exclusively by men, it can be assumed that what has gone on in court between men and women, and the decisions that have been made, are virtually undiluted by a woman's opinion. In the past, it was usually the man who stood accused, or was the defendant, against an aggrieved plaintiff. Today, however, the courts are becoming a battleground in the undeclared war between the sexes. When men are arrested for crimes against women, it is often rape, or assault with intent to commit rape, with which they are charged. In the civil courts, women seek material compensation or custody of children.

Let us consider some recent cases seen and how they throw light on current male attitudes.

In December, 1991, Mr Justice Ognall sat in judgement at Manchester Crown Court in the case of two sixteen-year-old boys who, together with a twelve-year-old boy, jumped on a fifteen-year-old girl's bed and held her down while raping her in a children's home in Tyneside. They left and returned later 'for seconds'. The judge freed the two older boys. Here is what he said to them, as reported in *The Independent*, when acquitting them:

'It is not necessary to lock you up in this unusual case. The whole of the evidence and your backgrounds demonstrate that neither of you were aware of the true gravity of your conduct. I do not dismiss the girl's ordeal lightly when I say you regarded it as some kind of prank. If you are daft enough to muck about with young girls again there won't be a second chance.'

It is difficult to know what was in his mind when he used those words. One wonders what his reaction might have been if the girl had been his own daughter, or his wife. The use of the word 'prank' may cast some light on his attitude. It conjures up images of healthy boyish fun, the sort of clean, rough behaviour we expect from boys. As such, it is perfectly acceptable, normal and understandable. And to send the boys away with an admonitory wag of the finger smacks of the sort of paternal chiding boys get if they break a window. Furthermore, do boys 'muck about' with girls? Is that how the judge views sex generally? When I was a boy, I mucked about with boats, catapults and sand castles. I didn't muck about with girls. I did try to have sex with some, and occasionally, if the girl was willing, I succeeded. It wouldn't have occurred to me to think I was mucking about with them. It just wasn't appropriate terminology. It is how we refer to casual preoccupation with objects that take our fancy for a while. We don't want to spend too much time with them, just to experiment for a while and then we move on to some*thing* else. It is precisely how some men view sexual relationships.

Was justice served or not? Did the judge feel that no lasting harm had been done to the girl? Most importantly, was the judge's decision a reflection of the subconscious masculine rebellion against the Women's Movement?

That's how it might have looked to many women in 1991 when an American Senate Committee ruled in favour of Judge Clarence Thomas, a black man chosen by President Bush to one of the highest offices in the U.S. judiciary. No sooner was he nominated than a female lawyer, who also happened to be black, Professor Anita Hill, accused him of sexually harrassing her some years previously.

Historically, when puritan America hears that her leaders indulge in illicit sex they can kiss their careers goodbye. So when Thomas was exonerated it was, if not technically a precedent, a decision that was certain to be taken into account in future cases.

What was particularly riveting here was that black was pitted against black for all America to see. It was no doubt most upsetting for those black civil rights campaigners who want to present a united front against whites. Yet Professor Hill was prepared to make a crack in the edifice for the sake of her sex.

A British judge had Thomas in mind when he directed a jury not to be influenced by that case when considering their verdict in the case of Houston v. Smith in October, 1991. Unusually, two doctors were fighting each other in court. Mr Justice Otton was summing up after hearing all the evidence. Dr Malcolm Smith claimed that Dr Alanah Houston, who shared a surgery with him, had accused him, in front of patients, of groping her staff. Apparently she had said: 'We have all had enough of you feeling our breasts, pinching our bottoms and brushing up against us.' Dr Smith took Dr Houston to court and won his case.

The judge's summing up might conceivably tell us something about his views when he used terms such as 'storm in a teacup', and he suggested that if the jury found in Smith's favour, that the award 'must not be miserly'. (In fairness to the judge, though, the Court of Appeal does say that the judge should describe the award thus.) After a long deliberation, the jury found in favour of the man.

In the previous year, a man of thirty-nine took a twenty-nine-year-old woman back to his place for champagne and she later accused him of rape. The man was acquitted by an Old Bailey judge who commented to the jury: 'When a woman says no she doesn't always mean it.'

That statement is critically important for it virtually guarantees that in some courts women will have no credibility at all in a rape case. It is a uniquely male point of view. No one even dreams of applying that principle to men, let alone using it to make a judgement. And to hear it in a court of law takes the breath away. It virtually sanctions rape. Any man who presses his attentions on a woman who says no, has been given the wink to ignore the word and plunge in regardless. Does the judge himself proceed according to the dictates of his own wisdom? If he wanted to have intercourse with a woman, would he forcibly push himself into her body if she resisted?

Consider, also, the most publicized and avidly watched rape trial of all time, that of William Kennedy Smith, the nephew of the late John F. Kennedy. He met Patricia Bowman in a bar and took her back to his home in Florida and she alleged that he raped her on the beach. What followed was probably the most sordid sexist spectacle in the history of the sex war. Basically, it was a tasteless display of American justice at its brassy and flamboyant worst. In the end it all boiled down to the skilful dismantling of a woman's credibility. In short, Smith was acquitted, and one trusts that justice was done. Many observers felt that the state prosecutor, the young and prim Moira Lasch, had handed it all to her opposite number, the experienced defence lawyer Roy Black, on a plate. The examinations and cross-examinations could not have been planned better to guarantee universal titillation.

Feminists are very bitter about this sort of treatment of women who report rape. It discourages rape victims from coming forward, they say, and they have a point. It is the same old story: men are unable to believe that any woman who goes out with a man can be raped; secretly, women *must* want it. The alternative – that a woman might reject a man's advances – is unacceptable.

And what of provocation? Englishman Stewart Porter

said he overheard his wife Nicola talking to her lover, Alan Ward, with whom she worked. Porter alleged that when he confronted her she taunted him about being 'useless in bed'. He flew into a rage and stabbed her twenty-four times with a knife before leaving their home in Edgware in London with a gun. He drove to Ward's house where he shot him to death in front of his family and his friends. He stood over Ward and refused to let anyone near until Ward died twenty minutes later. Porter's defending counsel convinced the court that he was out of control when he killed the two, and Porter was found guilty of manslaughter on the grounds of diminished responsibility. He was sentenced to nine years in prison, and presumably that will be substantially remitted if he behaves himself while inside. Said the judge: 'You were subjected to substantial provocation when she taunted you with her affair and your sexual prowess or lack of it.'

Now that's where it hurts, gentlemen.

It also hurts women when one of their own shoots the Movement in the foot. For men, it couldn't have come at a better time. On 9 November, 1990 a woman was jailed at the Old Bailey in London for twelve months for crying rape. It made headline news in the *Evening Standard*. Georgina Kyriakou, a thirty-year-old hotel receptionist accused a Lebanese man of raping her in her own room. He was arrested the following day and spent twelve days in custody because he couldn't speak English and the duty lawyer assigned to him advised him to keep his mouth shut in case he put his foot in it. Then, to everyone's surprise, she withdrew her allegation and admitted lying. Her defending counsel said she had sought comfort and assistance but hadn't got what she expected.

Why does the case leave me feeling very uneasy?

Of course, men don't have it all their own way in the courts. Women, too, can get off lightly. But they really have to suffer a lot to earn their dollop of male sympathy.

Consider the case of Pamela Sainsbury, who went to her husband's toolbox, took out a length of nylon cord, went to him where he slept in bed and strangled him with it. She tied one end of the cord to the bed, wrapped the other round his neck and began pulling. He woke up and started struggling, and she kept pulling. She hacked the body into pieces, put them in plastic rubbish bin bags and threw them over a hedge into a cornfield. The head she kept in the house for eight months before dropping it into the garbage to be carried away by the dustmen. Eventually she confessed to a friend.

The night she killed him, in September 1990 after a visit to a nightclub, he had thrashed her particularly badly, almost breaking her legs. It's worth going into the history of this case. It contains all the suffering of women rolled into one person's experience of violence at the hands of the rampant male who finds himself outclassed by a woman.

Pamela, a pretty, gentle-faced girl, had been one of the brighter girls in her school. A school prefect, she obtained ten O levels and two A levels, and wanted to be a laboratory assistant. In 1982 she met Paul Sainsbury in his home town of Sidmouth and they fell in love. He was a bricklayer with a passion for weightlifting. In 1983 their daughter Lindsay was born, but the trouble had already started. Paul got his kicks kicking Pamela. He was particularly annoyed when she used 'long' words that he couldn't understand. He wanted her to function at his own level, so he launched a campaign of humiliation that was to turn an articulate, intelligent woman into a near-silent creature who spoke only in monosyllables.

He thrashed her into submission and forced her to take part in his sexual 'games' and sessions of photography. He put a dog collar round her neck and made her crawl naked round their home and forced her to eat from a dog's bowl. He stabbed her with pencils and kicked her so hard the marks of his shoe were still imprinted on her body eight months after his very last kicking session. He used his fists, a strap and a cane. She never complained, but one night she killed him and she wrote in her diary: 'This is the first day of the rest of my life.'

The psychiatric reports were unanimous: she killed her husband while suffering from a temporary mental illness and she walked free.

What is one to make of all this? Quite simply, it substantiates the central thesis of this book, namely that the male who feels threatened by a woman will resort to physical violence. Men are providing the proof of it faster than it can be written down and published. The violence may not always be overt, but it is happening nonetheless. Men with sufficient sense to reason are learning, or at the very least being impregnated with a subliminal message, that they can beat up women and rape them and get away with it, not necessarily because rape is difficult to prove, but because of a trend towards anti-feminism. Men at every level, from bricklayer to judge, are becoming impatient with the new liberated woman. They are getting sensitive to having feminine freedom flaunted and celebrated before their resentful eyes. So they are reasoning thus: Okay, if that's the way they want it, that's fine by us. If they want to hunt in our tough world, so be it, and let's see how good they really are. We want to cherish our women, protect them and provide for them the way it's always been, and get our reward, which is a hot meal, a clean shirt and sex whenever we feel like it.

More and more, women are going to have to fight, and learn how to win against a strong, lusting and vengeful male. And the battleground in not only the beach, the bed, the office or the car, but also the courtroom.

This may be anathema to the caring man who wouldn't dream of attacking anyone, let alone a woman, physically. But just how well does the caring male know himself? It is conceivable that there is a gentler but no less effective weapon that he might resort to, perhaps unconsciously. The chances are, he has already used it. We call the weapon breach of contract.

In the jewellery business, a man's word is his bond. A dealer in precious stones would sooner cut out his tongue than lie to another dealer or go back on his word. He knows that if he did, he would make himself a pariah. Does this same man have a similar fanatical commitment to his agreements with his wife? Perhaps she doesn't have the same view of the contracts that he has. Basically, she doesn't realize that far from having a deal with him, she is part of the deal. Now, they are trying to get their names onto the dotted line, and men don't like it.

Life is structured around contracts. There is a case for arguing that all intelligent life is impossible without contracts. Furthermore, the first deals struck were almost certainly between the male and female of species varying from spiders to man. A contract was struck between male and female to permit copulation to occur, to ensure survival of the young and of the mother, and to ensure the successful development of the young after the birth. Those primitive deals were not and are not written down, but they are etched deeply into the brains of the parties involved; they are engraved in the genes.

As time went by the deal was extended to include interactions between males in order to allow them to behave co-operatively for the purposes of survival. Thus, two monkeys or lions can successfully displace a third from his harem provided they agree (a) not to attack each other at any time before, during or after the campaign; (b) to share the spoils; (c) collaboratively to protect their gains afterwards. Between humans, it is likely that the first all-male contract was made between the first two proto-males who cautiously raised hypothetical open palms to each other. They were making a contract not to kill each other. And if one looks carefully at various human transactions from that basic survival deal to the most sophisticated agreement between a man and woman to sleep with each other, we find that virtually every interaction between two individuals includes, and may depend for its success on, a mutually acceptable deal or contract. In fact, without deals, the normal functioning of human society would be impossible. They allow the flow of information, labour and resources. Strictly speaking, a deal is a good thing. It keeps men from killing each other over land, possessions and women. The deal, especially the written and signed deal, is a form of protection, a compromise, an agreement between two individuals free to make it. In some cases it is a compromise between freedom and safety.

So what is a contract anyway?

Legally speaking, a contract is an agreement giving rise to obligations enforced or recognized by law. The contract, generally, requires that both parties should have reached agreement, the agreement should be certain and final, and the contract can be enforced in law. The law isn't interested in the letter of the contract. What's written in it is not relevant. What is relevant, however, is how acceptable the contract is, morally and legally. It's the appearance of the contract that counts. For example, a pimp may have a very fair and equitable contract with a prostitute, but the courts would rule it invalid because it is an immoral relationship. On the other hand, a woman may sign on the dotted line to obey her husband and allow him to have sex with her whenever he feels like it. Unless she can prove he raped her, which is now an offence.

The courts are still largely of the opinion that a husband is entitled to expect reasonable access to his wife's body. And if she consistently denies him his statutory orgasm he could walk out of the marriage and hope for a favourable settlement. It's worth taking a close look at the interactions surrounding one particular contract, i.e. the one between a prostitute and her client.

9

Sex For Sale

Men buy sex. Women don't. It's a gender difference that is so obvious it cannot be ignored. As with all other aspects of male behaviour it goes back such a long way we shall never know how, when or where it began. It is, however, natural behaviour. Men are buying pleasure, not babies. This raises two important questions: why do men pay for it, and why do women, who are normally so fussy about whom they would accept as lovers, agree to copulate with a strange man for money?

It would be easy to say that men buy sex for the thrill of the orgasm, and turn to other questions. But it is not that simple. The giveaway is the question many a man who goes to a prostitute asks after he has ejaculated: 'Did you enjoy it?'

After all, why should he care? He doesn't ask whether the salesman enjoyed selling him a car. He knows from the indifference, boredom and patently faked orgasm of the prostitute that she regards him as a piece of passing meat, and yet he needs, not wants, to know that she was excited by having his penis in her body. Even the rapist sometimes asks that question. He is like the paying customer in that they are both taking their sex from an unwilling or disinterested woman, and yet they suddenly develop a blindness to the reality of the situation.

The answer is that they don't care whether she enjoyed it or not. All they need is the reassurance that they have the power to give a woman pleasure, and they are prepared to go into fantasy to get that reassurance. They are like the sneak lover or the man who creates the impression that he copulates often with women. They need to have a sex life, even if it means having to pay for it, or imagining it. It is so fundamental to the male that if all women insisted on payment for intercourse, men would pay up without a murmur. It would also, incidentally, abolish the whole concept of prostitution.

But it is not only the sneak lover who pays for sex. It is not just one particular type of man who buys intercourse. All sorts of men do it, from tough guys to weaklings, prime ministers to tramps. They may invent motives, ranging from curiosity to lust, but beneath the conscious desire is a deeper drive to etch into the world another notch proclaiming their manhood, their potency, their success as males, their ability to please a woman sexually. And prostitutes know this. After all, if all a man wanted was an orgasm, she would simply help him to achieve it. She does that anyway, but at the same time she gasps, grunts, heaves and writhes in simulated ecstasy. One woman told how when she masturbates a man she automatically starts breathing fast to simulate excitement, yet when he ejaculates she carefully aims his penis towards a conveniently placed wad of paper towels. He observes this and is left in no doubt that he has been handled as clinically as he would have been at the dentist. But the men, she says, keep coming back for more.

The paying customer may, in most matters, be a very smart fellow indeed. He may govern a country, rule a vast business empire, and be known for his burning intelligence. But put him in bed with a prostitute and he will be ready to believe her cries of orgastic agony. Does she really enjoy it? One prostitute tells how sickened she was when she accidentally had an orgasm with one of the punters. Another described how she has trained herself to study for an Open University course, mentally sketching out essays in English literature while her customers labour over her.

It's all a matter of self-discipline. One explained that the money kept her son in an expensive public school. She was taking money from men in order to train her son to be a man who might one day pay another prostitute to complete the cycle.

Obviously prostitutes view what they do as a job. It's a means of getting money in order to survive in a workplace dominated by men. As far as they are concerned, they have an agreed contract: pay up and you can have my body for a set time, whether you stick your organ in me or listen to jazz while looking at my body. Men, however, do not see it that way. They know they will have to pay for it, and the wise prostitute asks for and gets her money in advance. The customer, however, pays up with a sense of grievance. No matter that he knows he is visiting a prostitute, deep down in his soul he hopes that she will take one look at him and breathe: 'Wow, for you it's free.' But she never does and it's always a slap in the face. No wonder, then, that prostitutes fear their customers for the unreasonable rage that may flare up so suddenly and unpredictably. But the money is good, and they are prepared to take a chance. And there is no shortage of customers prepared to take out the short-term contract with a prostitute.

Men have laid down strict rules for the drawing up and defence of contracts with other men, and the courts are empowered to interpret these contracts and rule on their validity. In the light of the above, it is therefore ironic that the only contract that men take seriously with women, namely the fee for professional sex, is one which they rule invalid and illegal in the courts. Yet this contract has all the classic elements of the usual business deal. The customer, client, punter or call him what you will, agrees to pay a fixed price for a set amount of a woman's time. She guarantees in return to provide her body for his use; the terms of the contract are usually agreed in advance as to the extent of her services. The price depends not only on

151

the length of time given but on what the man wants. If all he wants is manipulation by hand to the point of orgasm he will not take up much of her time and the fee is going to be lower than that asked of a man who wants to spend an hour in bed naked with her. The deal is no different mechanically from that made between a market analyst or advertising company and their clients. Furthermore, like the successful company, she knows how to handle her clients.

Her greatest potential contribution is in understanding the human male. She has to be an expert in order to survive, since she deals on a daily basis with men whose fundamental nature has temporarily broken through the thin veneer of restraint. The skilled prostitute is not a trained psychologist, therapist or lion trainer, yet she successfully manages nature's most dangerous animal when all he has on his mind is copulation. And at the same time she actually gets him to pay her money. From the moment he walks into her life she begins to know him, his potential for violence, his danger signals, his real motive for visiting her. Every word she says, whether she knows it or not, is calculated to manoeuvre him into a frame of mind which will neutralize his anger, build his confidence, and thus maximize her safety. Her facial expressions, gestures and procedures are designed to get him in and out fast and uneventfully. She asks for the money immediately, knowing this is a source of rage, and from then on he can forget that he has had to pay. Also, it is harder to get the money afterwards.

She knows instinctively that virtually every man longs for the days when as a little boy his mother or nurse undressed him, stood him in the bath and washed him down with her own hands, how she tenderly lathered his backside, between his legs and his genitals, and so she does the same. She washes him, and by doing so takes him back until unconsciously he becomes again the little boy being washed by his mother. As a result, he is much more malleable. The bomb has been defused and her job will be a lot easier.

Thereafter it's horses for courses. He gets what he paid for, and if she takes pride in her work she sees to it that he gets satisfaction. As far as the quality of the service goes, it's like any other business. It all boils down to price. If he wants the best and the most variety, he must expect to pay higher prices.

During the work she dissociates herself from her body. It is a tool of the trade, a conveniently machined instrument that will do the job, a machine to be cared for since it is vital for business. Thus she will not hesitate to complain if he hurts her during intercourse. And in most cases he apologizes immediately and is more gentle.

No one understands men the way she does. She is, potentially, an enormously powerful weapon for their manipulation. This is appreciated by big business, by the armed and secret services and by governments, who have used prostitutes for as long as anyone can remember. Battles and countries have been won and lost, and reputations made and ruined, through the intervention of prostitutes in the pay of powerful men.

Social stigma prevents many men from knowing how available is the woman of their dreams. For a prostitute, through her understanding of men, has the power to provide a man with the closest he could ever get to the perfect wife. She has learnt what no other woman can hope to know as well: how to keep a man happy; how to dissipate the primal rage of the frustrated animal; how to satisfy him sexually; how to guide him through his life of male fantasy. And not only that, when he loses his job to a woman who does it infinitely better, a prostitute wife can make enough money to keep the whole family secure. Unfortunately the same drive that propelled him to a prostitute will prevent him from sharing her body with other men, and if he did marry her, it is possible that in the end he would turn on her, attack her and perhaps kill her. This is part of the price the prostitute pays for entering her profession: she virtually eliminates her chances of a white wedding. She has a lot working against her as a prostitute, and as her range of work options widens she will find it easier to leave the profession. If she does disappear, it is unlikely that women of the future will build a statue for her, but she will remain, nevertheless, one of the numberless millions of women who paid a higher price that anyone can ever know in order to help liberate the rest of her sex.

Her passing would not be good news for the human male who has to pay for sex, who would see yet another outlet for his fantasy, another corner of his macho theme park disappear. Who knows, he might perhaps have to turn to other men instead.

10
Man to Man

Long ago, before anything was written down, and when men and women lived in caves and rock shelters, the bigger, cleverer and more powerful men were the first to eat the meat which they had brought home and which the women had cooked for them. The lesser men of the group waited sullenly but quietly for their share. After all, they had not partaken of the hunt; they were stunted, crippled, lame, cowardly; in some cases they were women in all but shape. The only exception was the insane one, who grinned stupidly and spoke nonsense. His insanity was feared. The men of this elite kept themselves apart while eating, and when they had done with food they went to the very darkest recesses of the cave where the magic pictures of the animals were painted on the walls. No one else was allowed to see the pictures in case their magic was drained away and their power to draw the animals back every year to the hunting grounds dissipated. The men carried burning fat to the back of the cave where the light never penetrated. They took with them the young boys who were old enough to hunt, and who were shown the pictures and thus given the strength and courage necessary to fight and kill the animals. These men had formed a tight bond, a group which excluded all other males.

Those who contend that male bonding is built into the genes, and thus biologically necessary for the male to function normally, point to similar behaviour among other primates. Chimpanzees form hunting bands and so do baboons. In the wild, male baboons make friends with each other. Two or three males, usually the most dominant in a troop, join up and stick together all the time. They greet each other by presenting hindquarters in turn for fondling or touching. They do everything as a team, from procuring females for intercourse to fighting off lesser males who want to join the gang or copulate with the females, who, incidentally, are never admitted to the group.

These males take it upon themselves to guard the troop, stationing themselves as sentinels when on the move, and defend the others against predators. In human society, the police and army, well known for male bonding, take a similar protective role. Submissive primate males, just like men, want very badly to be accepted by the select group of dominant males and often present their hindquarters, hoping perhaps for a fondle. They may also be saying, Hey, don't worry, I'm no match for you, I'm just a nice guy. If we accept the theory that all males need bonding, then the failure to be accepted is bad for the animal's state of mind, be he man or baboon.

He may, of course, not need it at all. It has been argued (by a woman) that male bonding is a totally artificial, formalized arrangement between men who, lacking any real biological need to come together, create one in order to provide a justification for their own existence. Maybe. Women argue that if there is a sex that needs a biological bond to bring them together, theirs is it. After all, they bear the burden of the species.

As time went by, and as civilizations evolved, powerful men continued to form exclusive groups. Those with similar interests, occupations and fears realized that their needs would best be served by presenting a strong, united front to the world. Membership was limited and reserved only for those who could further the interests of the group. The aims of the group were dictated by the membership. They could be the furtherance of specific economic policies. Thus grain farmers, sheep and cattle farmers, and metalworkers formed their own specialized associations, to protect each other from the avarice of others. And there was no point in having weaklings in the group, since they would continually require assistance and protection and ultimately exhaust the group's resources. And there was no point in having women who could contribute nothing since they were barred from the occupations of men. In any event they would inflame and disrupt the tenor of things with their sexuality.

This prehistoric and historic scenario is reminiscent of certain forms of male behaviour today. It has in fact been faithfully carried through the millennia to the thousands of exclusively male institutions which exist throughout the world. It may explain why men still stick together, why they form clubs, associations, fraternities and secret societies such as the Ku Klux Klan and the Freemasons. They get together in pubs and other watering holes, and the most remarkable thing about these gatherings is the complete exclusion of women. In many cases women are not merely discouraged but are legislatively barred. Gentlemens' clubs have rules forbidding membership to women. Masonic lodges are strictly for men. They come together in groups of three or more to form special, intimate and jealously guarded relationships, excluding most other men and all women. They will admit a newcomer to the group, but only if the members recognize some special quality in him.

This is male bonding, and it is probably one of the most important phenomena responsible for the traditional suppression of women. Lest women dismiss the male fraternity as a joke, they should appreciate that the male bond has kept women out of all professional life for centuries, out of politics, sport, education, labour and religion.

These groups may be powers for good or for evil. The

Ku Klux Klan espouses racism, discrimination and violence. Unlike many male-bonded groups, it is *not* particularly exclusive, and accepts all males in the community who are prepared to swear allegiance. Other groups, however, are exclusive. In South Africa, the country has for years been run by a highly select and secret group of men, the members of the Broederbond. Outsiders know virtually nothing about the Broederbond – who they are, where and when they meet, and what they do. But it is very likely that their members include men who hold some of the highest positions in the country. They are probably all of Afrikaans stock, since one of the main if unstated aims of the Broederbond is to promote the Afrikaans culture and ensure that it survives, and continues to dominate the country in all spheres. Few doubt that the major policy decisions of the country originate behind the closed doors of the rooms in which the members of the Broederbond meet. There are, or have been, similar, secret groups in most other countries, for example the P-2 in Italy, the Thuggi in India, the Mende of Sierra Leone and all-male fraternities in U.S. colleges. It goes without saying that weaker males and all females are excluded from them.

Those who make it their business to watch men and women interact, and even those who do it as amateurs, will know that when women get together, even for the first time, their meetings are relatively free of the posturing and manoeuvres that blight those between men. When women meet they are aware of each other and not so much of themselves. They quickly establish mutually acceptable areas of conversation and shared experiences. They listen carefully, and will come away from the meeting able to repeat very accurately what the other people have said. Women are more likely than men to sit down afterwards and summarize the meeting in a diary. The astute business manager will always make sure that women attend important meetings with clients. Newcomers to women's groups are not expected to prove anything. It is rare for women in groups to differ in a damaging way, although if quarrels do occur they reverberate for years afterwards.

Men, on the other hand, often find it difficult to meet and communicate accurately. The problem can be seen in action in a pub, clubroom or at work. A strange man enters a pub and is clearly ill at ease, particularly if the others are huddled together at the bar. He feels or thinks he sees the eyes of the other men upon him, weighing him up as a man, and his resentment flares immediately. This will cloud his judgement instantly, which is a pity, since the other men didn't give him a second glance or thought, and would readily have made room for him at the bar. Consequently he broods over his pint in a lone corner or drinks up fast and leaves. Alternatively he may start a fight. Many a violent career in the American West was born in an imagined insult.

What he should have done, of course, was to stroll up to the counter, order a drink and start chatting. But even if he does this, he may still concentrate on giving what he thinks is an impressive performance, and will modify his posture and facial expressions, and possibly even his accent. This too, is a shame, since he will be so busy with trying to create an impression that he won't hear what anyone has said to him.

Many men feel that they stand a better chance of being accepted into a male-bonded group by demonstrating a desirable manly trait, or by picking a fight, or spending lots of money, or boasting. Normally they fail. What usually impresses men is what impresses women – honest achievement. The man who joins an advertising firm and quickly lands a good client is going to make more friends than the guy who buys all the drinks and loses a big client. The newly transferred centreforward who scores the winning goal will find the circle opening for him at the bar, and the glow he feels cannot be put down on paper.

A woman achiever might wonder why she is excluded from the male-bonded group.

There are some fundamental problems, as Rachel Hayhoe-Flint found out. As captain of the English womens' cricket team, she applied for membership of the MCC and was turned down. They haven't had a woman member in 200 years, and apparently don't intend to start now. Her achievement in cricket is not in doubt. Her problem is her sex. She is just not one of the boys.

When men get together they discuss women. They tell jokes, swear and disclose secrets about sexual adventures. Women would inhibit them. Perhaps that is what upsets the men at Lord's cricket ground, and the pub owners in Welsh mining towns who kept special lounges where the women had to sit and drink without their men.

Perhaps some women don't mind this enforced protection. But many do, and have pushed their way to the bar stool. They are also clearing a path to more important male preserves or hunting grounds such as politics, the police force, the armed forces, and wary male eyes are upon them. Despite man's difficulty with the concept of a policewoman or female soldier, it is in these areas, the most male of preserves, that men are showing that they can admit women into a male-bonded unit. Women are being admitted to the fraternity. Once they get past the sexuality barrier, men develop fierce comradeship with women who wear the same uniform. It can work. The uniform helps because the difference in basic body structure is minimized. The problem is that when women do make it into the group they may become unwomen, alter-men. When you join the group you can't play at being a man, you have to be thought of as one. Either way, women have to do most of the adjusting.

In some institutions no amount of adjusting seems effective at present. Arguably the most potent and enduring male-bonded groups can be found in the City of London. These are the ancient guilds of London merchants which have never admitted women and don't seem likely to start now. Within these guilds, the attitude towards women, in particular the wives of guild members, is benevolent in the extreme. Wives are loved, honoured, cherished and thoroughly spoiled. Special nights are arranged when wives and guests are permitted to dine with members and enjoy the pomp. Women connected with the guild benefit in many other ways. These are powerful men, and they can do much for their wives, daughters and nieces. Many a door can be opened and favour obtained and the wise woman exploits these advantages while sticking rigidly to the rules that say 'Don't cross the line'. But that apart, women are kept well away from the administration of the guild. This is male bonding with a vengeance. If women were able to break into membership of the guilds they would be doing very well indeed. If they can't they will continue to face a formidable barrier to full sexual integration.

There is also another type of male bonding which proves that men can overcome the barriers to male-male interaction at an intimate level, and one which might provide important tools not only in understanding men, but in freeing men from the prison into which they have somehow locked themselves. The type of male bonding to which I refer is homosexuality.

Some might argue vehemently that homosexuality is not male bonding, which involves the formation of exclusively male groups, but a sexual relationship between two men. This is not the case. It is a meeting of minds, not just of bodies, and involves groups of people not just two individuals. It is, nevertheless, a bond between men which excludes women. It is as natural a form of human interaction as that between man and woman and unless homosexuality is studied openly as a characteristic of the human male, we shall never fully understand him.

Very little is known of the history of the subject because few men wanted to write openly about it, and because in many cultures the study of homosexuality was socially and legislatively suppressed. In addition, homosexual men would not bring their homosexuality into the open for fear of jeopardizing their careers. Over the centuries, homosexuality came to mean different things depending on who was thinking about it. In the beginning, it was probably accepted as just one more expression of erotic and sexual interaction between individuals, and in some human societies still is. But in others a moral dimension was introduced, and homosexuality was deemed abnormal and immoral. This led to a third major view; that of the legislator, who made homosexuality among men illegal.

Antagonism among men to homosexuality goes back a long way, at least to Roman times. The Greeks, however, were appreciative of beauty in the human male, and thus today we speak of an Adonis or an Apollo. Homosexuality was an acceptable part of life in ancient Greece. The evidence is that Greek heterosexuals enjoyed sexual intercourse with boys as much as they did with women. The Spartans, who placed much value on military life, thought it was better to take your lover to the wars rather than leave one behind at home. In early Islamic writing one finds a tolerance for homosexuality, and beautiful men were greatly prized. Homosexual men were viewed as different types of men. A moral judgement was made, however, in that love of men for wives was 'passionate but good', while that for men was 'passionate but bad'. This was written in the tenth century by one Saadia Gaon, a Jewish historian who lived and worked in a predominantly Muslim society. In most early cultures, erotic love that did not produce young was viewed somewhat askance, even if practised heterosexually.

In mediaeval Europe, gripped with religious madness,

homosexuality became more than just another sin of the flesh and lumped as such with heterosexual intercourse. This antagonism developed into fanatical hostility. Homosexuality, the moralists pronounced, could be contagious and had to be contained. Possibly this stemmed from the fear of latent homosexuality in the individuals who made these judgements. From about 1400 to 1650, governments and the Church in Europe attacked homosexuality with vigour and men were executed if it could be proven that they were practising homosexuals. Churchmen themselves were not immune from persecution – an Anglican bishop, John Atherton, was hanged for adultery, incest and sodomy in 1640.

And yet during the period in Europe that saw persecution of homosexuality, there flowered in art an idolisation of the human and particularly the male form that is appreciated to this day. Artists, notably Caravaggio, Michelangelo, Rafael and Donatello set men on fire with their representations of men, both mortal and divine. This in itself would have been sufficient to create a moral dilemma. It is analagous to modern media messages about the female form. Men are encouraged to admire the image of a provocative woman on a vast billboard, to watch simulated and occasionally real copulation on a cinema screen, and simultaneously warned: look, don't touch. Inevitably, some Renaissance men touched.

While Europe rejected homosexuality in other parts of the world it had been legal and considered sexually normal, for example in Japan, China, New Guinea, the Australian Aboriginals, some African tribes, and among the North American Indians. In China, the homosexuality of Aidi, the last emperor of the Former Han Dynasty, has been documented in the *History of The Former Han*. In China, as in many other countries, homosexuality was acceptable provided men also carried out their reproductive duties. But during the seventeenth century homosexuality became a national preoccupation, and in 1770 the Manchu Quing government made sex between consenting males illegal.

Curiously, female homosexuality did not arouse the same passionate response. As long as women did not make a spectacle of themselves, and did not humiliate the men, they were left to get on with their own sexual preferences. Also, women were not as educated as men. They did not have the opportunity to publish their sexual behaviour. While hundreds of men were executed annually in Europe for homosexuality, prosecution of women for this was virtually unknown. During the sixteenth century, for example, there were only ten convictions in the Netherlands, Italy, Spain, France, Geneva and Germany collectively. And if a woman was punished harshly, it was not so much for her sexuality as for offending men. Take, for example, the case of the nun Sister Benedetta Carlini of Pescia, who was given life imprisonment in about 1620 for enticing her cell-mate to masturbate her. She had visions, she claimed, which demanded this. In that case, men were outraged not by lesbianism but by blasphemy. A clue to the indifference of men to lesbianism is provided by the fact that men reacted violently only if they felt the woman was passing herself off as a man. Thus, a woman was burned at the stake at Fontaines in France, in 1636, for marrying another woman and playing at being the husband. In Spain, in the fifteenth century, two women were flogged and sent to the galleys for having sex 'without an instrument', whereas two nuns who used a dildo suffered the fate of any woman attempting actual penetration, namely burning at the stake. Woe betide any woman who takes away from the male that which is most fundamentally his.

From 1700 onwards in Europe, the movement against male homosexuals gathered momentum. Attitudes were hardening, and homosexuals began to be depicted as deviant effeminates of low or non-existent morality, and in 1892 the term 'homosexuality' was introduced into the English language by Charles Chaddock. This was possibly more damaging than any legislation, because it created a third sex, regardless of the sex of the homosexual. People were labelled, and once classified, were attributed with the stereotypical image whereby homosexuals have since been pilloried in the media. Prior to the label 'homosexual', men had considered themselves free to have intercourse with others of either sex, although some were more discreet than others about liaisons with same sex individuals. But the label changed all that. It is one thing to be thought promiscuous or sexually active, quite another to be called homosexual.

Homosexual men in the twentieth century have adopted another label, and call themselves 'gay'. It is an interesting choice. It is innocuous, inoffensive, entirely stripped of aggression. Yet it is still a label, and it will continue to divide rather than unite, even if it has provided a public rallying cry for the homosexual man and woman.

Homosexuality is a natural component of male sexuality. As long as it is an interlude, and not a way of life, it is acceptable to many men who would be aghast at any suggestion that they are homosexual. Shared sexual experiences are common in boarding schools for boys in Britain and in any other country in which they are run. More boys than would admit it have experienced some form of foreplay or actual intercourse with fellow pupils or masters during their school career. In many cases, it occurs in a dormitory containing other boys who are aware that it is going on. It is fair to assume that most of these boys have gone on to marry, bear children and lead 'normal' heterosexual lives.

Similarly, homosexuality is practised in prisons, military academies, ships, monasteries, YMCA dormitories, anywhere, in fact where men are deprived of women. And it would be naive to assume that the men who indulge never had or never will have sex with women.

Homosexuality as a sexual experience is therefore not as unacceptable to men as the Church and 'straight' society would have us believe. It is the image that it evokes that is so abhorrent; the implication of persecution, the resorting to surreptitious behaviour, and the anticipation of rejection and revulsion that stay the hand of the heterosexual.

Now, also, there is the very real fear of contracting HIV and AIDS. In the 1992 Wellcome Trust study of sexual lifestyles in Britain, it was found that only 13.7% of heterosexual men who had had more than five sexual partners within the last five years were attending clinics for sexually transmitted diseases, whereas 51.4% of homosexual men were attending. A microscopic virus may succeed where a virulent society has failed, in eliminating what evidence tells us is normal male sexual behaviour.

11
Hawks and Doves

When a few bacteria get together in a bowl of meat broth they start multiplying at a terrific rate, because conditions are so benign for them. There is space to spread out, good food, and no competition unless another type of bacterium also drops into the soup, particularly a hostile invader, or unless something else happens to the bacteria to lessen their fitness for survival.

So it has been with males. From the moment they emerged in the bowl of primeval soup called earth they multiplied in numbers and grew in strength, in knowledge and in fitness. Nothing has successfully opposed their rise to power over the earth and all the other creatures on it. No other species has challenged their superiority, and unless they destroy themselves in wars or through disease, they are able to expand into the rest of the universe.

Until now, that is. Now a competitor threatens to stop the male dead in his tracks. That competitor is the human female, who wittingly or not has declared her intention of joining him aboard the intellectual rocket he is riding into the future, and perhaps he feels that there may not be enough seats on board for them both. A struggle has broken out for those seats, and for harmony's sake the seats have to be counted, and both males and females reassured that there is space on board for everyone. For this is one ride neither sex can survive on its own. Both sexes have to learn the cost of fighting for seats. And there is a way.

Hawks and doves is a game developed by John

Maynard Smith to describe strategies for survival in evolutionary terms, and it may be applicable to what is happening between men and women at the moment. Originally introduced to describe economic behaviour in human societies, game theory has extended into, amongst others, the disciplines of biology, warfare and government. Using very simple arithmetic, it is possible to gauge approximately how useful a particular strategy might be. It could tell the player if a particular strategy could lead to extinction. Maynard Smith introduced the game of hawks and doves in order to predict the outcome of animal contests, and since this whole book is about an animal contest, it seems appropriate to see whether some of his ideas might help men and women to realise just how dangerous a 'game' they are playing.

In order to keep things simple we will make sweeping assumptions and treat males and females as if they were two very uncomplicated organisms, competing for a single resource, namely the world. Secondly, up till now men have been the hawks and women the doves. So let's keep it that way as we play the first game.

A hawk attacks. He displays his intention to attack, then goes right ahead and does it. He escalates from display to attack, and stops only when the opponent retreats or when he, the hawk, is injured. The dove displays, but never attacks. She retreats as soon as her opponent escalates.

This predicts the outcome of any meeting between hawks and doves. Let's say the earth teems with men and women in exactly equal proportions, and furthermore that there is an equal chance of bumping into either a man or a woman, and that all meetings are encounters between a single man and women.

When they do meet, three different types of encounter are possible, namely man–man (M,M), man–woman (M,W) and woman–woman (W,W). All three have very different outcomes. The game tells us what they can expect to win or lose. When man meets man there's a fight. Neither backs down, and each has a 50% chance of winning or losing. That's a big risk to take. The victor takes all, less the costs of fighting, which means that the loser comes away poorer, perhaps lighter in pocket, minus his country, or nursing a broken head. When a man meets a woman, it's no contest. She doesn't even try, but backs away. Consequently, the man has no chance of losing, and she has no chance of success. He takes all the spoils, and she comes away empty-handed. But she loses nothing either. The encounter hasn't cost her anything. When woman meets woman, they may display, and look threatening, but neither actually attacks. In each encounter they divide the spoils equally. Consequently, neither is hurt and both gain something. So let's score the game.

Suppose that when players meet for the first encounter they bring with them a bag filled with their initial stake, something called their 'fitness points'. This is an apt name, since the potential cost is loss of life or limb or possessions. We label those fitness points (F_0), which will be slotted into a sum later on.

For man and woman let F_0 before the first confrontation equal +100 points.

After the encounter, players come away with what they have won, which we call V (for victory), or minus what they have lost, or limping with the injury they sustained. Let's call the cost of losing C.

Let injury have a cost C. Let C equal –5 points.

Let victory (V) score +10 points.

Victory and cost taken together constitute what we call the payoff, or E.

That is virtually all we need to know, except for how to play. And that is pretty easy. We set up the various possible interactions in graphical form, using a matrix. If, like me, this at once arouses a determination in you to flee

	MEN	WOMEN
MEN	$^1/_2$ (V-C)	V
WOMEN	0	V/2

	MEN	WOMEN
MEN	+2.5	+10
WOMEN	0	+5

Figure 1. The matrix for the hawk-dove game. The top matrix shows the formulae for calculating the payoffs, and the bottom matrix shows the payoffs for victory (V) = +10, and cost (C) = –5.

the game, don't. What follows is painless (unless you're out there fighting).

The matrix shows the possible types of meeting, and how to calculate the payoffs for the various players, depending on whom they run into. The players are listed down the side of the left, and their opponents above and to the right. The payoffs (E) from the game are shown in the first matrix (Figure 1).

When two men meet, the payoff will be:

$$E = ½ (V - C)$$

The ½ represents the probability of meeting another man. Since men and women are around in exactly equal numbers, that probability is ½ or 50%, or 0.5. Men cannot hope to carry off all the spoils without injury. Victors and losers may limp away from a fight. Thus the cost is deducted from the payoff.

When man meets woman, he has no cost. She has no victory, nor does she incur a cost. So he gets V, she gets 0.

When woman meets woman, they split the spoils equally. Thus, for them, the payoff (E) equals V/2.

Three points arise from the matrix:

1. The female always retreats before the male, who gets a payoff (E) of +10 without injury. The female's fitness therefore is unchanged *in an encounter with a male.*

2. In a contest between two females, they share the victory, i.e. they each come away with a payoff (E) of +5, and no one gets hurt. A dove always increases fitness after an encounter with another dove.

3. A male vs male contest results in a 50% chance of getting a payoff (E) of +10 and of getting injured, which is also a payoff.

Let's now develop the situation to apply it all to all men and women, bearing in mind that I am making some massive, simplifying assumptions, such as that all men have equal power, that all women have equal behavioural responses, and that neither sex can deviate from the game plan.

What we do next is to calculate how man and woman have changed the fitness they brought to the first game.

Before the first game, everyone had +100 fitness points. To find out how many each has afterwards, simply add up all the possible combinations of payoffs and add them to or subtract them from the initial fitness.

Thus, for men, initial fitness $F_0(M)$ equals +100.

For women, initial fitness $F_0(W)$ equals +100.

Remember, also, that there are equal numbers of men and women in the world. In other words, the frequency (p) of hawk-like men and dove-like women, is equal, or 50%, or p equals 0.5.

In one contest (i), from the matrix in Figure 1, let the payoff for a man be:

171

$F_1 (M) = F_0(M) + p \times E(M, M) + (1-p) \times E(M,W) \ldots\ldots\ldots (1).$

Here F_1 is the fitness in points after the game, p is the probability of meeting either a hawk or a dove, and E is the payoff.

Substituting figures from the matrix,

$$F_1 (M) = 100 + 1.25 + 5 = \underline{106.25}$$

Therefore, man (hawk) increases fitness by 6.25%.

Let the payoff for a woman be:

$F_1 (W) = F_0 (W) + p \times E (W, M) + (1-p) \times E(W,W) \ldots\ldots\ldots (2)$

Substituting figures from the matrix,

$$F_1 (W) = 100 + 0 + 2.5 = \underline{102.5}$$

Thus, to summarise,

$$F_1 (M) = 106.25$$
$$F_1 (W) = 102.5.$$

(Notice that to get the payoff in each case, we have to multiply the payoff by the probability of meeting either a hawk or a dove.)

Therefore, men gain 6.25% from any contest, while women gain 2.5%.

Using compound interest, and multiplying by 100,000 years and by the number of contests, men clearly win hands down – men win the world.

Furthermore, they keep it. Maynard Smith also introduced the concept of what he called an evolutionarily stable strategy, or ESS, which is one likely to keep the species extant. We know we have an ESS if we beat all other players in the game. Thus, women don't have an ESS on their own. From a survival point of view, being a dove is not an ESS. A pure population of doves is at risk through invasion by hawks. Tahiti man is an example: if a belligerent gang of men were to land on the island he would get his throat cut. Human history is littered with extinct tribal populations whose friendly waves were swept aside by an invader's sword. Thus, if men are turned from hawks into doves, and not enough women turn from doves into hawks, then the human population would not have an ESS. Women are not exempt from this terrible law.

If this earth was populated by only dove-like women, everything would be fine until a spaceship filled with men landed. They would take over immediately, and at the very least enslave the women. And that is more or less what has happened.

Plainly the real situation is very much more complex than this simplistic scenario suggests, and I could advance more equations to show that I have left out some important factors. For a start men and women do not behave so uniformly as bacteria. But I have made the point, and anyone who wants to savage my sums can refer to Maynard Smith or consider how history substantiates the validity of the result. The model does explain how it is that women, as doves, didn't and wouldn't ever stand a chance of beating men – unless men and women together *change* the game.

If women are to redress the balance, they have to complicate the equation by being hawks sometimes. In fact, those female hawks are up in the sky and circling; and this means that the fateful value of p, the ratio of males to females, of hawks to doves, is changing. And the nature of the payoff is changing as well.

In the old game, as described above, as long as the victory (V) payoff exceeds the cost (C) payoff, or, to put it mathematically, if V>C, then we have an ESS.

Under these conditions, being a hawk is an ESS, since

the benefits of attack outweigh the risks. Sure, you are going to lose some hawks, or they are going to need patching up after the fight, but the net result is a gain.

If, however, conditions change such that the cost payoff exceeds the victory payoff, or if V<C, as may be the case in a war between men and women, then being a hawk is not an ESS. Nuclear warfare provides another example. The cost payoff would exceed the victory payoff, which is possibly the only reason why war has not broken out yet. (Generals also play this game.) Under such conditions the population would go extinct. The cost payoff will increase as more and more women desert the ranks of the doves and become hawks, especially if men remain hawks and fight. Without going into the maths., it can be stated that if V<C then for an ESS we should need a situation where the proportion of hawks should be V/C. In other words, the numbers of allowable hawks depends on the trade-off between the victory and costs payoffs.

This, however, is more easily said than done. Given the changes taking place right now the rules of that ESS don't apply; and it might be argued that at the moment there is no longer an ESS for men and women. Unlike bacteria, humans seem to have the power to choose strategies, and that is a very dangerous situation – the wrong choice, such as pressing the nuclear firing button, could spell extinction, not only for humans, but for the bowl of soup as well.

There are, however, other ways in which men and women could evolve an ESS, and they may be in the process of doing it right now, without realising it. The ancient drives to survive may be protecting us, steering us towards an ESS.

For the wild card in the game is the fact that women are bringing a new dove into the game, a sort of modified dove that Maynard Smith calls a retaliator, which expands and complicates the matrix. The retaliator acts like a dove with another dove, but escalates if the hawk escalates,

	hawk	dove	retaliator
hawk	$^1/_2$	V	$^1/_2$(V-C)
dove	0	V/2	(V/2)-1
retaliator	1/2(V-C)	(V/2)+1	V/2

	hawk	dove	retaliator
hawk	−10	20	−10
dove	0	10	9
retaliator	−10	11	10

Figure 2. The matrix for the hawk-dove-retaliator game. Here, the victory (V) = +20, and the cost (C) = −40.

which he always does, and a game can be worked out to take the retaliator into account.

The matrix for such a game is shown in Figure 2. Here, the retaliator behaves like doves with doves, and like a hawk with hawks. Since both men and women could be retaliators, I now drop the sexual terminology. From now on there are hawks, doves and retaliators.

The same scoring system applies, except that, in keeping with Maynard Smith's model, the retaliator scores slightly better than a dove in an encounter between the two, and the dove, conversely, loses slightly. In the example provided, the cost payoff far outweighs that of victory, which seems more realistic. The relevant formulae are shown in the figure. In even a cursory examination, it looks bad for a hawk, which is now up against not only other hawks, but the retaliator as well. Let's see what it does to fitness.

Using equations (1) and (2), and assuming:

(1) Hawk, dove and retaliator all come to the first game with +100 fitness points; and,
(2) The frequency of hawks equals 50%, or $p(H) = 0.5$; the frequency of doves equals 25%, or $p(D) = 0.25$, and that of retaliators equals 25%, or $p(R) = 0.25$ (not too far remote from the situation in human society today); then

For the hawk:

$$F_1(H) = F_0(H) + pxE(H,H) + pxE(H,D) + pxE(H,R)$$

substituting numbers from the matrix,

$$F_1(H) = +100 + (0.5x{-}10) + (0.25x20) + (0.25x{-}10)$$

$$= +100 + (-5) + (+5) + (-2.5)$$

$$= \underline{+97.5}$$

In other words, no gain in fitness; hawks actually lose fitness.

For the dove:

$$F_1(D) = F_0(D) + pxE(D,H) + pxE(D,R) + pxE(D,D)$$

substituting numbers from the matrix,

$$F_1(D) = +100 + (0.5x0) + (0.25x9) + (0.25x10)$$

$$= +100 + 0 + 2.25 + 2.5$$

$$= \underline{+104.75}$$

Doves gain in fitness.

For the retaliator:

$$F_1(R) = F_0(R) + pxE(R,H) + pxE(R,D) + pxE(R,R)$$

substituting numbers from the matrix,

$$F_1(R) = +100 + (0.5x{-}10) + (0.25x11) + (0.25x10)$$

$$= +100 + (-5) + 2.75 + 2.5$$

$$= \underline{+102.25}$$

The dove comes away from all encounters unscathed. The retaliator improves fitness but sustains some injuries. The hawk is on the way to extinction. We do not need it anyway; we have retaliators to look after us. Together, doves and retaliators represent an ESS (Figure 2). It means that doves and retaliators can share the resource, in this case the earth. The hawk, who wants it all, will not get it if faced by doves and retaliators. If we are evolving our society towards doves and retaliators, then, if the game we have just played is anything to go by, we are on the right track. The hawks will eliminate themselves, unless they switch to being retaliators, or doves. Anyone who wants to take the time to find out just what proportion of doves and retaliators are needed for an ESS can spend some time slotting in different values of p for hawks, doves and retaliators.

Finally, there is one more player to introduce, the one Maynard Smith calls the bully. It is worth bringing this player into the game, since bullies, both male and female, have surfaced in the gender war. The bully is a mixture of hawk and dove. It escalates a conflict, but retreats as soon as the opponent escalates. The bully always loses to a hawk or a retaliator, but always defeats a dove, and always shares its spoils with another bully. We can play the game again, this time with hawks, doves, retaliators and bullies, in order to find out how the bully affects the distribution of the resource, and just what impact it has. The matrix which takes the bully into account is shown in Figure 3.

If we assume that all players come to the game with +100 fitness points, and that there are equal frequencies of all players i.e. p = 0.25 in all cases, then at the end of the game, after adding up all the payoffs and adjusting fitness, the score table will stand as follows:

1. Hawk fitness: <u>105 points</u>

i.e. 100 + (0.25x–10) + (0.25x20) + (0.25x–10) + (0.25x20)

2. Dove fitness: <u>104.75 points</u>

i.e. 100 + (0.25x0) + (0.25x10) + (0.25x9) + (0.25x0)

3. Retaliator fitness: <u>107.75 points</u>

i.e. 100 + (0.25x–10) + (0.25x11) + (0.25x10) + (0.25x20)

4. Bully fitness: <u>107.5 points</u>

i.e. 100 + (0.25x0) + (0.25x20) + (0.25x0) + (0.25x10)

According to the model and the numbers chosen for this game, the bully has a successful strategy. Bullies and hawks together would comprise an ESS, as would retaliators alone. I know which I would prefer.

Just how relevant is the game to what is happening to men and women? The situation is changing rapidly, and both hawks and doves could be on the increase. Perhaps sex and gender will become unimportant as the species evolves towards increased fitness and an equilibrium, or

	hawk	dove	retaliator	bully
hawk	$^1/_2$(V-C)	V	$^1/_2$(V-C)	V
dove	0	V/2	(V/2)-1	0
retaliator	$^1/_2$(V-C)	(V/2)+1	V/2	V
bully	0	V	0	V/2

	hawk	dove	retaliator	bully
hawk	−10	20	−10	20
dove	0	10	9	0
retaliator	−10	11	10	20
bully	0	20	0	10

Figure 3. The matrix for the hawk-dove-retaliator-bully game. The victory payoff (V) = +20, and the cost payoff (C) = −40.

towards extinction. If as a result of losing the game males shut down and stop producing sperm, the females will have won the final Pyrrhic victory. In other words, the future of the human species may depend not on what men or women do about it, but on what happens to the male. Perhaps they have the right idea on Tahiti. Perhaps what is needed is a variation of *their* game, in which doves are joined by retaliators. The alternative scenario can only be an escalation of violence.

12
One Less War

Violence and power are two fingers of the same glove. The glove is worn by the victor, and in the case of many species the glove belongs to the male. Where a victory has been effected, the violence ceases and the practice of power can proceed peacefully. This power is exercised in the home, at the workplace, wherever the male and female meet. But when individuals or groups of the vanquished come together and rise in revolt, the violence flares up and the battle for power recommences. So it is with the human male and female.

Violence cannot occur without a predisposition, that being aggression. It is the expression of aggression, and it can be of a physical or mental nature. Among other species, we have evidence for physical violence only, and rarely between male and female of the same species. But among humans, violence is commonplace in both mental and physical forms. What is not known is whether it is the male or the female which is innately the most aggressive. Among other species, aggression may be more marked in the male, associated with sexually dimorphic physical features such as the horns of a bull, the antlers of a deer or the spurs of a cockerel. But some females, such as the gerbil, hamster or vole, which do not differ much in appearance from the male, are equally or more aggressive. Another aggressive female, the lioness, does the hunting for the pride, and needs enormous strength to chase and bring down her prey, which she does with legendary violence, as does another big cat, the cheetah.

Male and female aggression may be seasonal, associated with competition for the female, the protection of the nest and of the young. Thus the neural apparatus for generation of aggression is present in the male and female brain, and may not require the presence of a hormone to activate it. Some scientists feel that aggression and its expression cannot be activated without the male sex hormone testosterone. Certainly the removal of the testes renders a bull or cockerel docile. The castration of seasonally aggressive males such as the red deer deletes their aggressive behaviour. And the human eunuch was not a valued warrior.

It is also possible that testosterone, or one of its hormonal metabolites, was necessary during foetal development in order to organize and lay down the neural substrate for aggression. Reference has already been made to girls born of mothers who suffered from congenital adrenal hyperplasia, or whose mothers took contraceptive pills well into pregnancy. These daughters received abnormally high doses of androgenic steroids during critical periods of brain development, and claims have been made (and refuted) that these girls showed typically 'male' aggressive behaviour.

But it is just as easy to argue matters another way. It is quite possible that aggressive behaviour itself boosts testosterone secretion. Take, for example, a number of male rhesus monkeys and put them together to form a new group. Fighting will quickly break out as they work to establish a satisfactory hierarchy. Those males who are defeated will suffer something like an 80% fall in circulating testosterone concentrations. It happens to people too. Simply winning a tennis match can raise testosterone levels. But just in case one is tempted to seize on testosterone as an index of aggression, it should be pointed out that the human male can exhibit unmistakable aggressive behaviour before the age of three, when testosterone levels in plasma are insignificantly low. Other studies, however, support the theory that human males are 'more' aggressive than are females. A study carried out in a psychiatric hospital in Washington found that acts of aggression were predominantly made by men. Men, too, react more aggressively to bereavement. Due, however, to the evolution of very similar male and female human brains, and thus to a liberation from the constraints of the genes, it is likely that there is little to choose between the two sexes in the potential for the expression of aggressive behaviour. Any differences that we find between the sexes in this respect may be superimposed on natural inclination by society.

There is little doubt that boys play rougher games than do girls, be they North American or Kalahari San. Boys are encouraged to be aggressive and to demonstrate physical strength while in girls it is greatly disapproved of. Children, whether boys or girls, view female aggression as totally inappropriate. There is in virtually all human societies an enduring tradition, and it is no more than that, that perpetuates a cultural stereotype for the male and the female.

Ironically, the human female is welcomed as a spectator of aggression and violence. But active involvement is not expected. There is no means of proving that the female brain is programmed to be a spectator, but there are plenty of examples to support the statement that the female takes this ancilliary role on board, in some cases with considerable enthusiasm.

When the Zulu impis of Southern Africa went out to do battle with other tribes, they left their kraals with the ululations and cries of their women ringing in their ears. For centuries in many primitive societies the men have been whipped into murderous frenzy by their women. In fact, it would have been unthinkable to venture against another tribe without first being stoked up to white heat by the women. Rarely, however, did the female take up arms, although there are exceptions. In Dahomey, in West Africa, the king kept an army of several thousand women who served as a personal bodyguard, and whom he frequently sent against his enemies. By all accounts they were as ferocious in the field as any male battalion. The North American Apache female was as fascinated with violence as the male, although she did not join the war party. She would, however, take part with apparent eagerness in the torture of captives, helping to dismember them while they were still conscious. In modern western societies, women encourage violence. The custom of passing a man the white feather of cowardice was practised by English women until relatively recently. American prostitutes offered free sex to soldiers before they left for Vietnam. Violent sports such as boxing, wrestling and the martial arts have no shortage of ardent female supporters, and from an early age girls are now increasingly taking up body contact sports hitherto considered an exclusively male preserve. Both terrorists and their victims agree that female terrorists are as ruthless and calculating as their male colleagues.

In the face of this anecdotal survey, one can present statistics for the incidence of violent crime which show that the overwhelming majority of offenders are men. In the United States, until 1969, over five times more men than women were arrested for murder, and in the decade from 1980–1990 a quarter of a million Americans had died violently, 90% at the hands of men. In Britain, until 1984, at least ten times as many males were convicted for crimes of violence. In homes the world over, the male is seen to be the violent partner. Domestic violence, like rape, goes largely unreported, and comes to light only when it becomes sufficiently overt to attract the attention of the health or social services or police. It is a phenomenon virtually unknown among other species. It has been estimated that in America alone about two million husbands or wives are battered annually by their partners.

For centuries, and in very many human societies, the right of the human male to 'punish' his wife has been inscribed into the very foundations of the group. The practice persists to the present day, and the male's assumption that he has a biological and socially accepted right to punish his mate is prevalent in societies of both eastern and western hemispheres. It also highlights a point made in another chapter, that the male, once he has successfully courted and obtained his mate, completely changes his perceptions of her within his sphere of influence. And in this, he appears to be supported by other men. For example, in a study made of wifebeating in New York, 90% of a group of women interviewed reported that the police were unable to make an arrest. Two-thirds of the women claimed that the police were unhelpful. It appears, incidentally, that the western male wife beater is at odds with himself. Over 90% of those who beat their wives have a drug or alcohol problem. The wifebeater probably comes from a home in which he saw his own mother beaten by his father.

The wife may not accept that her husband has a right to abuse her physically, but she submits to it and co-operates with the male in keeping it a secret. In fact, most wives who suffer beatings stay with their husbands. This, of course, may be a matter of economy, apart from the complicating factors of love and offspring. Here again, one immediately faces the question as to whether women are programmed to accept such treatment. There is at present no evidence to suggest that this is so; it is more likely that women, due to their dependence on the male, and to their adherence to ancient traditions, are unable to put an end to their mistreatment by moving out or fighting back.

But, as we have seen, things are changing, and changing too fast for the male to cope with. The forces that kept the wife in the home are weakening. Women are crossing the threshold to work. They are generating income. With this new power they are expecting a bigger share in the decision-making process in the home. Coupled with this, the male finds his own source of income threatened, particularly as he gets older, due to a vast increase in the available pool of employable people (women), and he is put on a short fuse. Not only will he resent his wife *and other women*, but his health will begin to suffer. Stress will diminish his testosterone concentrations, and his libido will attenuate and he'll know it. His sperm count will fall. He will be forced into a job below his educational or experience-linked attainments, and this may increase his chances of heart disease. Already some men are leaving home to escape a situation so at odds with their inbuilt sense of maleness. In these homes the abuse rate is high.

What are we to make of all this? It is possible that as women get more power, so they generate more violence towards them from the male. Certainly, they are treading on his toes with a very heavy foot. His response is highly predictable, given his history of dominance. On the other hand, as women gain more equality, especially in the home, so may violence wane. One wishes this more optimistic view is the correct one. There is, however, no strong evidence for it. It is more likely that as women consolidate they will become more prepared to fight back.

Power can be many different things. Among other species it is the hard-won claim to a tract of territory, corner of a lake or to a harem of females. It is usually wielded by the male. It seems the female doesn't have the strength, nor apparently the inclination, to compete. She submits to male domination and in some cases enjoys several benefits related to physical safety and a constant supply of fresh food. In human societies it is far more complex, reflecting the multi-faceted nature of the group. But whether power be held by an elephant seal or by a man, it consists of the same elements and contains the same ingredients. These are:

1. The inequality of the male and female. He is strong. She isn't. He is not limited by a cumbersome reproductive life. She is. This makes him, in her eyes, very important for her own survival. If they are human this makes him, in his eyes, more valuable than she is. Many women fall in with this notion. Thus they submit willingly to man's power. He is, therefore, entitled to get more money for what he does than she can ever hope for. This principle has been so firmly cemented into the system that in western societies it can be countered only by legislation. A law has to be passed that says women deserve the same pay as men for doing the same job.

2. Just as the nursing female fox depends on her mate for food, so the nursing human female depends on her husband for shelter, warmth and a full refrigerator. This reinforces his opinion of his greater worth and the wheel of inequality is kept turning.

3. No matter how strong and insistent the male of any species is, he will not succeed in bending the female to his wishes if she doesn't want his attentions. He may rape her, but that will not secure her compliance. For it is her compliance that starts the wheel turning in the first place. She allows herself to be dominated by the male, and in the case of the fox it is the right move. She would starve otherwise. Women have been no less compliant for as far back as anyone can remember.

4. The other half of the equation is the male. The male needs to be dominant. It is how he evolved. Nothing changes. In all other species, the male who has dominated continues to dominate. Both male and female recognize the differences that establish the inequality and are content. It is only the human male who is watching his foundations crumble under his feet. The human male's need to dominate cannot be underestimated. He dominates not

only women, but children, other males, other animals from dogs to circus lions, and has even tried to dominate the weather. He is therefore non-selective. It is this drive for dominance or power that provides the energy required to keep the wheel of inequality turning. Power is expressed in terms of behaviour, not only of the male, but of the female as well.

In human societies, men have always been the hunters, the warriors, the pathfinders and land clearers. The women have been the direct carers, the domestics. The men have taken the greater risks, and because of this have claimed responsibility for making the decisions. There was some sense in this. They felt they needed to control the risks as far as possible. Thus power devolved to them. But women have taken power in some spheres. This was and still is of an informal nature. The laws have always been unwritten. Women control the resources, directly by apportioning food, and indirectly by dictating to the men what they must produce to ensure that women will buy it. This power is extremely limited and goes largely unrewarded by society. Some underlying principles have been recognized, and they go some way towards explaining why women have complied with men over the power imbalance.

Basically, there are three possible differences between the human male and female that could explain the imbalance. Firstly there is the biological differential. This has been explored in some detail in other chapters. Male and female are constructed differently. Men are assumed to be bigger, stronger, more aggressive, more intelligent and logical, and are programmed to dominate. That man possesses the first two 'advantages' is unarguable. There is no evidence for the other claims.

Then there is the behavioural differential. Men and women have different roles and adopt them through convention. They behave the way they are expected to. The pressures to conform, both from within themselves and from society are huge, and anyone who deviates from the expected pattern of behaviour will create a strain both at home and abroad.

Arguably the most important factor is that men and women may actually see the world differently. In other words, there is an ideological differential. In some ways this is related to the biological differential, but it can arise through a learning process. The ideological differential applies not only to the individual but possibly to the way society as a whole should be viewed. If both behavioural and ideological differentials are practised, as they are, for example, in the Middle East, then conflict between the sexes is unlikely to arise. Male and female recognize the differentials and are apparently comfortable with them. Deviation from them is dealt with swiftly and sometimes ruthlessly. Men and women need each other to maintain the differentials.

In western societies, women are expected to see the world the same way men do; they must, however, behave differently from men, because that is how previous men have arranged things, and how previous women have allowed things to be arranged. It is recognized by both sexes that if the behavioural differential were to be abandoned, both sexes would survive, but at the cost of stepping on the toes of the male. As long as the less dominant group (women) stay within their own sphere of influence, no conflict can arise. Women may exert their informal power in the home. If they stay there they stand less risk of losing that power. Within their own sphere, women are permitted to express their power violently. Women in a harem have killed other wives or their offspring in attempts to gain or retain power, without any danger of retribution in a male-dominated society.

Women have learnt how to survive the male. They have learnt how to avoid conflict. There are certain signals that protect the female from the male, just as there are manoeuvres for survival among other species. The animal who rolls over to expose the vulnerable under-belly, or who plays dead, will probably be left alone by an aggressive black bear. Similarly, both men and women (especially women) have developed signs to show that they accept the dominance of the male. These are non-verbal signals, and have been described in terms of sight and touch. The male will stare directly into the female's eyes. She is expected to drop hers demurely, or glance up at him through her lashes. The male will touch her, and she is expected to yield by leaning towards him, or softening against him. If he points a finger, she moves in the direction he is pointing. He frowns, and she responds with a smile. When they talk, he interrupts and she immediately stops talking. These signals, incidentally, also pass between boss and employee. When a woman starts using the 'dominance' signs on a man, she is virtually declaring war on him. She is making a bid for leadership. There is bound to be trouble.

In some other primate societies, leadership is invested in the most powerful male, and he has the run of the females. Even in less organized groups, such as the male deer and his harem, the females will follow where the male leads. It is unlikely that we shall identify instances in nature where the female is making a bid for leadership, except in human societies. Women, even powerful women, are fighting an inbuilt reluctance to take power and assume leadership. In laboratory settings, dominant women have chosen a man to lead the group. It is as though they expect leadership to belong to a man. Women exhibit a residue of the behavioural rigidity that keeps the female of other species in a submissive role.

But it is a small residue. Women are picking up the weapons of the male, and are attacking on several fronts. The question is, can the male change fast enough to accommodate change? Let us see how he responds to large-scale liberation of women.

Consider an hypothetical third world country. The men have been seduced through the infiltration of western culture into relaxing their tight hold on women. They have allowed women to start working and to make and break some of the rules that govern their society as a whole. Women have severed the bonds that tied them to purdah, or the harem, or to a hut. They have begun to displace men from powerful jobs and are revelling in their new freedom. All seems to be going well. But under the surface the male temperature is rising. This is not the western male, who seems prepared to backpedal all the way, but a man who has been accustomed to absolute rule, whose traditions are steeped in the lore of masculine pride and invincibility. Slowly he realizes what he has done. He gets together with other men and they start talking. These women are going too far. This was supposed to be a game, a flirtation with western-style democracy, a little glamour in the office. But look here, the women are pushing themselves everywhere. Now they are starting to tell us what to do.

So, one day women wake up to find that there has been a coup. Men have taken charge again, determined to put things right. Women roll up for work, only to be turned away and told to go back home where they belong. Resistance is futile. Men are stronger than women, remember, and what is more the army is happily backing the government on this one. But the men don't intend stopping there. It's time women went back to concentrating on their principal duties, namely breeding sons and keeping their men comfortable and sexually satisfied. Clearly a tighter rein is needed, especially over female reproductive activity. Men want more sons, and from now on they will take a hand in getting them. And they have the means to do it. And the knowledge. For western science has given them all the information they need in order to control the female population.

Firstly, all women who have attained high positions, especially in government, are liquidated as traitors to the new Glorious Revolution of Womanhood. Lesser female leaders are exiled with five year contraceptive implants of progestagen to ensure that they do not propagate any more leaders. All women are informed that they must register with the euphemistically named Family Planning Centres where their reproductive cycles will be charted through regular blood sampling. Oral contraception is obligatory for all unmarried women and extramarital sex punishable by death for both partners. When a woman falls pregnant the sex of the foetus is determined, and if it is going to be a girl, the woman is made to take a single-dose oral abortion pill if the birth of her daughter will mean exceeding the quota of women allowed for each month.

It may sound like a far-fetched scenario. Perhaps, but in some countries attempts by women to change the restrictive status quo might well precipitate a violent collective male response. Ironically, the scientific knowledge that women consider has helped to liberate them can also be used to bind them even more tightly than before.

In western countries women have gone to a lot of trouble to evaluate themselves and their position in society. They have also put the male psyche under a microscope. Armed with this information, they have formulated methods to alter their perceptions of themselves, to change the male attitude and to abolish the social and statutory limitations which have barred them from leading full, satisfying lives. Strategies have been worked out to enable women to enter and succeed in the world of men. They are teaching themselves how to cope with male violence. They are working to change the male attitude to women. And they are making extraordinarily rapid progress on all fronts.

But they have not yet undertaken an in-depth analysis of how their struggle for liberation will affect the male. For affect him it will. And, as has been repeated so many times in this book, those effects will not advance the cause of the human female.Women cannot wait for men to sit down and analyse themselves to the same extent. Men just don't go in for it. They analyse society as a whole and produce plans for operating their society, but they don't know anything about themselves at all. Contemporary journalism reveals the male's reaction when attacked verbally by the female. For example, in an article entitled 'Badmouthing' in the Sunday Times magazine 9 December, 1990, Neil Lyndon complains about abuse directed at the male. Among others, he quotes Julie Birchill: 'A good part – and definitely the most fun part – of being a feminist is frightening men.' This quote is singled out because it says a lot about present male–female relationships. This canny woman knows that men are frightened. And his article proves it. It is anything but masculine. It is plaintive. The author comes close to getting down on his knees and begging for mercy. The female scents victory.

Ms Birchill's apparent attitude is as destructive as that of the Victorian physician quoted earlier. She should be thinking about the fun she'd have helping to bring men and women to a common purpose. She might suggest that men start learning more about themselves. But that isn't the way things are going. If anything, the war of words is hotting up.

There is more than one way to hurt people. The male relies on fists, feet, hammers and his penis. Women turn to words. This is of course a generalization and it reeks of sexism. Many male authors are superb wounders in print. But it is possible that while doing this they are using the female side of their nature. There is no doubt that when women write about men, their pens are wielded like daggers and their fingers are hammers pounding their anger, frustration and resentment into the body of the male. Scarcely an issue of a good newspaper or periodical appears without somewhere in its contents a scorching attack on men. Women have mounted an assault on all fronts. No sphere of society has escaped criticism. Education, the arts, science, politics, religion, you name it, women have found men wanting. Even a cursory glance at the papers leaves one with the uneasy feeling that something very violent is brewing out there. Women have found a weapon and they are using it. It is a very good weapon, for they have right and logic on their side. But, regrettably, the pen could well be knocked aside by the sword. Let's see what a few of the women are saying.

Possibly the most virulent book I have come across so far is *Misogynies* by Joan Smith. The cover depicts two naked women being engulfed in the feathers of a huge bird, presumably a cock. The tone of the book is angry. The theme of male exploitation of women burns its way through the book from beginning to end. Women are shown to be mere articles, held in amused contempt by men, tolerated and to be used like so much merchandise. It is also a catalogue of the wrongs women have suffered at the hands of men. Much of what is written in *The Fragile Male* is consistent with what Ms Smith has found. She has aimed the book like a rifle. But it is not clear to me whether she will hit her target, namely men. I bought it because it was relevant to my thesis. But when I showed it to other men they shrugged it off as hysteria. As is the case with so many books about men by women, it will be read, perhaps almost exclusively, by women. A kinder and more comprehensive book is the work by Dr Rosalind Miles entitled *The Rites of Man*. She, too, looks for an explanation for the aggression and violence in the male and uses a potent mixture of science, literature and psychology to explore its expression through the ages. It is a pity that her book will probably be read by relatively few men.

Men, it seems, are not interested in reading about themselves, particularly when the author is a woman. Most men can handle titles such as: How to Develop a Super Power Memory; How to Seduce a Woman; Body Language and Making Sales and so on. But they don't want to know about failure, especially their own. This hasn't stopped women from writing. Perhaps they feel that if enough of their own sex read critical articles and books they will be spurred into action. This is a more realistic aim.

Possibly the most frequent target of women writers is the media treatment of the female. Television in particular is regularly blasted by female critics who find many programmes deeply offensive to women. In an article in the Times on 30 November, 1991, Lynne Truss ran through a series of programmes which dealt with interactions between men and women, and her tone was a mixture of bewilderment, anger and amused scorn. It would be interesting to see the credits for many of the programmes she mentioned, since many producers are women, women who have to achieve certain ratings in order to keep their programmes and jobs.

It was therefore fascinating to learn that ITV brought out an all-women chat show, chaired by the news editor Eve Pollard. That is quite an achievement, you say; we can get across the female viewpoint to men at last. Well, perhaps, if men are prepared to wait up until 3 a.m. to watch it. At the very least men could video it and watch later. The producer, Dee Maclure, must have been thankful to have taken her programme out of daytime television. The subjects covered included just about everything that women are expected to be interested in i.e. parenthood, sex, diet, fathers, dress and childlessness. It is no wonder that the programme is scheduled for 3 a.m. No man wants to watch that, unless he eats quiche. It must rankle, if you're Eve Pollard, unless you don't mind perpetuating the image. How about discussing business, masculinity, seduction, sport and science? There is a good opportunity here to reach the half they want to reach, or do the producers want only women viewers and panellists who can fire their bullets aimlessly into the air?

It is clear from what is appearing in print that women are far more interested than are men in finding out what is going on between the sexes. Men, on the other hand, plough on with studies of the body. In the fields of physiology, psychology or disease, there is a marked imbalance favouring research into the female (a point also made by Mr Lyndon). It is not the remit here to ask why this is so, but to draw attention to it. Hopefully men will start redressing the imbalance, for not to know yourself is to lose yourself.

What can be done to defuse the war of words? Generally speaking, the most constructive thing would be to open the lines of communication between men and women, to cut away the layers of misunderstanding. This is no easy task, given the pressures of sexuality that come between men and women and their attempts to relate on an intellectual level. But an attempt must be made. There are societies devoted to steam trains, stamp collecting and bee keeping. There should be societies dedicated to bringing men and women together to work towards a common, mutually helpful philosophy. These societies should publish widely, use the media often, and spread the good word world-wide. It's what advertisers do so well.

It *is* starting to happen. You can buy a book entitled *Men, Masculinities and Social Theory*, which contains the proceedings of a conference attended by men and women to address the problem of the modern male. Apart from a few acrimonious passages it appears to be an honest attempt by men and women to get together to find some common ground.

It is easy to make suggestions and a darn sight harder to

try to put them into practice. But in the light of the problems raised in the previous chapters, some courses of action do come to mind which rely on the premise that the male, even if he cannot eradicate the hunter within him, can learn about himself. He has to be taught from an early age that there are no differences in aptitude between men and women, despite the obvious sex differences. This means that teachers have to be trained first. Therefore the science of gender studies has to be developed and fast. It is no use having a vast, well-stocked library devoted to women's studies and a few books here and there documenting the evils of the male. We should aim to know and understand the male and female and teach them about themselves from as early an age as possible.

It seems ludicrous that there is no formal education to prepare men and women for family life. Two people who previously lived only for themselves are suddenly thrown together and expected to make a go of it. You may as well toss an untrained medical student into the casualty ward. It is no wonder that about one third of all marriages in most western societies end in divorce, usually before two years of marriage have elapsed. How can two raw recruits be expected to cope with a brand new human being without even one hour's worth of tutoring? Surely we need state-funded family centres where everyone gets a decent grounding in how to succeed at life.

It is high time that the missionary instinct was revived. And it will be dangerous work. Men in many other parts of the world have not yet been challenged. True, in China and Russia women have been liberated to work, but if one looks closely at what they do, it seems that they have been freed to be just as low in status as are men. Furthermore, during times of high unemployment in those countries women are encouraged to go back into their homes and breed, and may even be penalized if they don't. Of course, men are making those decisions. They still have the power.

The world is a big place, and contains billions of men and women. Very few of those live in the countries in which the gender upheaval has occurred. In Western Europe and North America thousands of people are studying the sociology of gender interaction, and are coming up with ideas, many of which are drawn from other, sometimes very primitive societies. Their ideas occasionally generate powerful responses and progress is made *in Western Europe and North America*. But for three-quarters of the world's population there is no machine with which to make the necessary changes in attitude.

It seems unlikely that the practices of infibulation, female circumcision, polygamy or claustration could penetrate the coccoon which western women are spinning round themselves and their men. Yet it is dangerous to believe that all those people and their ideas and influence will remain in their own parts of the world forever. Their cultural ideas and practices are quite capable of spreading west, and who knows what gods we shall be worshipping tomorrow.

Man will always give to the world his two gifts of beauty and death. He will struggle with his left hand and his right. He will always want things from women. Sometimes he will win them and sometimes he will take them. That is his nature. It will never change for man, and if it does change he no longer will be man. Some presidents will continue to steal from their own countries and rape their women; some members of parliament will forge passports and abscond with funds and their secretaries, some male Church of England ministers will stand in pulpits and preach the word of God and seduce their female parishioners. We should not be surprised; they are men after all, driven by forces that will not be denied. Men will press themselves up against women in the Underground trains and commit frottage, then go to work where they will play the violin, design new buildings and write papers on saving the environment. We should not try to pretend that he is something he is not.

The biological imperative is inflexible. Sexual function and behaviour for most species is fixed and invariable. And so it should be, since any small variation could result in extinction. Most males on earth don't have a chance against their genes and their hormones. Neither do the females. This creates a form of harmony that lasts as long as the species does, as long as no mutations occur. Most males and females enact their roles blindly, with no consciousness of dissatisfaction in those roles, and no sense of injustice. Humans alone have complicated their sex lives through intelligent discrimination, and the result is a disturbance of the reproductive equilibrium. Men can no longer function as untrammelled males, and women seem to them to be taking away what little they have left. If this continues, the consequences are unpredictable but likely to be worse rather than better for both sexes. Fortunately, humans can reason, can temper their actions with judgement and can act collectively. However collective reasoning may not always produce a happy result.

Some of the more extreme members of women's groups have suggested that men are expendable. It is exceedingly likely that in the near future techniques will have been developed to culture human testicular seminiferous epithelium indefinitely, and harvest and store the spermatozoa it produces. The genetic contribution of the sperm will be determined once scientists have successfully characterized the human genome or genetic database. Women will know that they are being inseminated with sperm which carries no communicable (inherited) diseases, although they will have less, if any, control over the latent psychological input contributed by the sperm. The only real problem is that a boy might result, although even that would be controlled, since biologists are now well on the way to finding all the sex-determining genes.

Laboratory simulation of the human male reproductive system is not a far-fetched fantasy. It would be far more difficult, on the other hand, to recreate artificially the female reproductive system with its complex cyclical activity of hormone production and follicle maturation, and the intricate foetus–placenta–mother unit. If one sex were to survive, it would more likely be the female. There is no evidence, biologically, that the human species is on the way to parthenogenesis, but medical research is busily creating the tools to replace the slower evolutionary process.

Of far greater immediacy are the social implications of changes in sex dominance and gender pressures. There has already been much speculation about the future of the male–female interaction in all spheres of social life. Several suggestions and scenarios have been suggested. It is doubtful whether any of them are practicable since all involve radical changes in the self-image either sex has of itself, individually and collectively. Conscious decisions have to be made about defining the qualities, aims, strengths and weaknesses of the group and to amend these in order to expand the group to admit new members. In other words, men and women should work towards ironing out differences which in the past have stimulated discord, conflict, exploitation and open warfare. Some of these changes are already taking place, instigated mainly by the male under pressure from the female. Women are getting more power outside the home, they are entering into every form of occupation previously considered the sole preserve of the male. They have become increasingly liberated from their own reproductive systems. Oral contraceptives, tablets to induce abortion and hormonal treatments for postmenopausal symptoms have broken many of the bonds that tied women to the home. It is now possible for a post-menopausal woman to be rendered fertile and have a baby if she wants it. Women should now feel sufficiently confident to relax about men and sit down with them and work towards preventing glorious revolutions for either sex. Women should not hope for what some call the New Male to suddenly appear.

Women talk about the New Male, they write about him and they despair when he seems to be as far away as ever. They may have to wait a very long time, for the New Male is a myth. He is the product of collective wishful thinking that has resulted in a designer male who will make the streets safer at night, sweep away the biological, sociological and ideological conflicts between men and women, and usher in a New Age of intersexual peace, harmony and equality. Women will have to wait for a long time, since nature makes her changes very slowly and the next version of the human male may not be quite what they had in mind.

It would be far better to make the most of the male who is around at the moment. True, he is a wild, dangerous and uncontrollable animal, but he is also capable of creating a world of such beauty as is beyond the descriptive talents of any craftsman of words. We have only to look around us to see the expression of his inner beauty and to realize that the world would be a drab place if he were suddenly to depart, leaving behind him only an inexhaustible supply of A-grade sperm.

But he is not going to leave us now or in the future. He is going to continue to enrich the world with his art and science. He will make women happy and miserable and he will not deviate from his violent and destructive ways. Man is a fact of life, there is no changing him either through books or laws, and women can either come to terms with this or intensify the sex war. E. B. Taylor, writing in 1871, said: ... 'Our thoughts, wills and actions accord with laws as definite as those which govern the motion of waves, the combination of acids, and the growth of plants and animals.'

Taylor's words underscore a central theme of this book – that the human male's thoughts, wills and actions are driven by forces outside his control. If man can accept that fact, there is hope he can use his intelligence to straighten out his attitude and behaviour towards women. If men and women together can use their vast store of biological knowledge to tackle gender conflict both inside and outside the home, gender inequality could become a thing of the past.

It will be no small task and it will be expensive. But if we can find billions of pounds to dig holes between England and France, or to make strange luxuries like Concordes, we can find the cash to create a new school subject – the study of gender – and train people to teach it.

That would only be a start for if men and women do succeed in understanding themselves better, there will still be trouble. After all, we're all human. Blood will flow and wars will rage. Crime will flourish and people will savage each other in the workplace. But if men and women work together to try to carry us forward on our slow and painful journey to peace, it will be that much easier; one less war to fight.

Glossary

adrenogenital syndrome Excess production of androgens by female adrenal, resulting in hirsutism, acne.

anabolic steroid Substance which adds muscle mass e.g. testosterone.

androgens Substances acting like the male sex hormones, producing male-like characteristics.

anthropology Study of human societies.

asexual reproduction Reproduction not involving gametes. Offspring genetically identical to parent are produced.

axillary hair Hair under the arms.

Bar Mitzvah Ritual for Jewish boys aged 13 who must read a portion of the Torah (Old Testament) in Hebrew before a congregation of men.

blastocyst Implanted fertilized egg.

bushido Code of the Samurai.

circumcision Removal of the skin covering the glans penis.

claustration Covering up of women, guarding and chaperoning them; hiding them away (see **purdah**).

couvade Father mimics mother's childbirth ordeal.

cuckoldry Fooling others (usually males) into nurturing one's own offspring.

diploid Possession of two sets of chromosomes.

dowry Price paid by bride to bridegroom.

ejaculation Emission of sperm by the male at orgasm.

endocrine gland Gland secreting hormones directly into the blood stream.

epiphyses Ends of the long bones; when they seal, growth ceases.

epithelium Sheet of cells lining external or internal surface in multicellular organisms.

evolution Process of genetic change in a species.

fellatio One individual sucking the penis of another.

fertilization Combination of male gamete (spermatozoon) with female gamete (ovum).

follicle Group of cells acting as a reproductive unit e.g. the ovarian follicle produces the ovum or unfertilized egg.

frottage Masturbation by rubbing up against something.

gamete A cell containing one set of the genes e.g. sperm or ovum.

gender Manifestation of sexual identity.

gene A unit of inheritable matter, made up of DNA.

genetics Study of mechanism underlying heredity.

genotype Genetic database of a particular species.

gonads Testes or ovaries.

haploid One set of genes of an individual (contained in the gamete).

heterosexual Sexual preference for opposite genetic sex.

homosexuality Sexual preference for same genetic sex.

hormone Chemical released by an organ, which affects other organs.

HRT Hormone replacement therapy during and after menopause.

hummel Male deer without horns.

hypothalamus Area at base of forebrain, controls sexual function.

impis Zulu battalions.

implantation The attachment of the fertilized ovum (morula) to the endometrial lining of the uterus.

infibulation Sewing up the labia minora.

labia majora Large folds of skin, usually covered with hair which enclose the other structures within the pudendal cleft.

labia minora Smaller folds within the labia majora; sewed up for infibulation.

lek A place where males congregate to display for the female.

libido Sexual and aggressive energy; according to the psychoanalyst Freud, it is contained within the so-called 'id'.

lobola Payment by African bridegroom to bride's family.

lordosis Curvature of the spine; a posture adopted by rodents when sexually receptive.

macho Tough, male image.

mahu Homosexual Tahitian man offering fellatio and sodomy to other men of village.

meioisis Division of a diploid cell into two daughter cells, each containing a set of the genes of that species.

menopause Cessation of ovarian activity in women; ovulation ceases, accompanied by mood changes and 'hot flushes'.

mitosis Division of a diploid cell to produce more diploid cells.

monogamy Formation of pair-bond between single male and female, excluding others of either sex.

moran Masai boys undergoing initiation into manhood.

morula Fertilized ovum before implantation.

mutation Change in genetic database.

neonatal Newborn.

neurone Nerve cell.

oestradiol Female sex hormone, secreted by ovaries and to lesser extent by adrenal gland and testis.

oestrogens Substances acting like the female sex hormone oestradiol.

oestrous cycle Cycle of sexual rhythm in animals which do not menstruate. Controlled by oestrogens, female will accept males only during oestrus phase of the cycle.

oestrus Period when female of certain species are sexually receptive to male.

oocyte Unfertilized egg.

oral contraceptive (OC) Drug or combination of drugs taken by mouth to block pregnancy.

osteoporosis Weakening of bones due to loss of calcium; occurs after menopause through loss of oestradiol.

ovulation Rupture of ovarian follicle to release ovum into oviduct.

parthenogenesis Independent growth and development of unfertilized egg.

pituitary Gland at base of brain; secretes hormones that control the gonads and adrenal and thyroid glands.

plaeomorphism More than one form.

polyandry Female mates with more than one male.

polygamy In human societies one husband taking more than one wife.

polygyny Male mates with more than one female.

postnatal After birth.

prenatal Before birth.

primordial Primitive.

proceptivity Indication by female to male that she is sexually interested; the 'come-on'.

progestagen Progesterone-like drug; usually used in oral contraceptives.

puberty Start of reproductive competence in boys and girls.

purdah Hiding away and veiling of women.

receptivity Female prepared to accept male for copulation; prepared to allow him to insert penis.

Samurai Japanese warrior.

semelparity Once-only reproduction; parent dies after fertilization or after laying eggs.

semen Fluid ejaculated by male at orgasm.

seminiferous epithelium Tissue within testes that produces spermatozoa.

sexual reproduction Genetically unique offspring produced by fusion of male and female gametes.

sodomy Anal sex.

spermatozoa Male gametes produced by seminiferous epithelium of testes.

subincision Slitting the underside of the penis to create a 'vulva'.

testosterone Male sex hormone, secreted by Leydig cells of testes, and to a lesser extent by the adrenal gland.

vagina Passage into which penis is inserted.

viviparous Offspring develop inside mother's body.

vulva Also called the pudendum; female external genital organs.

wand-nat Term for masculinity used by Amhara tribe.

Bibliography

References for each chapter are given, and recommended reading is starred with an asterisk. Occasionally, direct reference to a specific newspaper article is given in the text. However, since there are few sources given in the text, I have indicated specific topics in parenthesis after certain references to direct the reader to the relevant source.

Chapter 1. The Coming of The Male

Much of this chapter is my own speculation. I did, however, draw heavily on the well-known and influential work of Fisher, Muller, Parker and Trivers, whose theories on the advantages of sexual reproduction, the origins of the gametes, gamete size and on the male–female contribution and commitment to the reproductive process are consistent with my excursion into prehistoric guesswork. Also, I used much of what is known about the promiscuous and ranging behaviour of existing males to construct my proto-male.

*Ammerman, R.T. and Hersen, M. Current issues in the assessment of Family Violence. In: *Assessment of Family Violence*. Eds R.T. Altman and M. Hersen. Wiley, New York, 1992. p 3. (Estimate of wife-beating incidence in USA.)

*Archer, J. and Lloyd, B. *Sex and Gender*. Cambridge University Press, 1988. Chapter 3.

Betzig, L. 'Mating and parenting in Darwinian perspec-

tive'. In: *Human Reproductive Behaviour*. Eds L. Betzig, M. Borgerhoff Mulder and P. Turke. Cambridge University Press, 1988.
Daly, M. and Wilson, M. *Sex, Evolution and Behavior*. Wadsworth, California, 1983. Chapters 1 and 2.
*Darwin, C. *The Descent of Man, and Selection in Relation to Sex*. D. Appleton & Co, New York, 1871.
Fisher, R.A. *The Genetical Theory of Natural Selection*. 2nd revised edition. Dover Press, New York, 1958.
Journal of the American Medical Association, 1990. 14, pp 264. (Female medical student intake.)
Muller, H. J. 'Some Genetic Aspects of Sex'. American Naturalist 1932. 66, pp 118–138. (Advantages of sexual reproduction.)
Muller, H.J. 'The Relation of Recombination to Mutational Advance'. Mutation Research 1964. 1, pp 2–9.
Parker, G.A., Baker, R.R. and Smith, V.G.F. 'The Origin and Evolution of Gamete Dimorphism and the Male–female Phenomenon'. Journal of Theoretical Biology 1972. 36, pp 529–553.
Trivers, R.L. 'Parental Investment and Sexual Selection'. In: *Sexual Selection and the Descent of Man*. Ed. B. Campbell. Aldine, Chicago, 1972.

Chapter 2. A God On Earth

*Buruma, I. *Behind the Mask: On Sexual Demons, Sacred Mothers, Transvestites, Gangsters, Drifters and Other Japanese Cultural Heroes*. Pantheon Books, New York, 1984. (Japanese men.)
*Gilmore, D.G. *Manhood in the Making. Cultural Concepts of Masculinity*. Yale University Press, New Haven, 1990.
Herdt, G.H. *Guardians of the Flutes*. McGraw-Hill, New York, 1981. (Sambia-fellatio.)
Herdt, G.H. 'Fetish and Fantasy in Sambia Initiation'. In: *Rituals of Manhood*. Ed. G.H. Herdt. University of

California Press, Berkeley, 1982. pp 40–100. (Sambia rituals.)

Hill, W.W. *An Ethnography of Santa Clara Pueblo*. University of New Mexico Press, New Mexico, 1982. (Pueblo Indian boys.)

Lee, R.B. *The !Kung San: Men, Women and Work in a Foraging Society*. Cambridge University Press, 1979. (Bushmen manhood ritual.)

Levine, D.N. 'The Concept of Masculinity in Ethiopian Culture.' International Journal of Social Psychiatry, 1966. 12, pp 17–23. (Amhara tribe.)

Murdock, G.P. *Culture and Society*. University of Pittsburgh Press, 1965. (Men and women: table of work.)

*Saitoti, T.O. *The Worlds of a Masai Warrior: An Autobiography*. University of California Press, Berkeley, 1986.

Thomas, E.M. *The Harmless People*. Vintage Books, New York, 1959. (Bushmen rituals.)

van Gennep, A. *The Rites of Passage* translated by M.P. Vizedom and G.L. Caffe. University of Chicago Press, 1960. Originally published 1908. (Principles of puberty rites.)

Chapter 3. To Make a Male

Beach, F.A. 'Sexual Attractivity, Proceptivity, and Receptivity in Female Mammals.' Hormones and Behavior, 1976. 15, pp 325–376.

Geschwind, N. and Galaburda, A.M. 'Cerebral lateralization. Biological mechanisms, Associations, and Pathology: I. A Hypothesis and a Program for Research'. Archives of Neurology, 1985. 42, 428–459. (Brain lateralization and testosterone.)

Gorski, R.A., Gorden, J.H., Shryne, J.E. and Southam, A.M. 'Evidence for a Morphological Sex Difference within the Medial Preoptic Area of the Rat Brain.' *Brain Research*, 1978. 148, pp 333–346.

*Goy, R.W. and McEwen, B.S. *Sexual Differentiation of the Brain*. MIT Press, Cambridge, 1980.

Herrenkohl, L.R. 'Prenatal Stress may Alter Sexual Differentiation in Male and Female Offspring.' Monographs in Neural Science, 1983. 9, 176–183.

Imperato-McGinley, J., Peterson, R.E., Gautier, T. and Sturla, E. 'Androgens and the Evolution of Male-gender Identity among Male Pseudohermaphrodites with 5α-reductase Deficiency.' New England Journal of Medicine, 1979. 300, pp 1233–1237.

Keverne, E.B. 'Olfactory Cues in Mammalian Sexual Behaviour'. In: *Biological Determinants of Sexual Behaviour*. Ed. J.B. Hutchison. John Wiley and Sons, Chichester, 1978.

*Laycock, J. and Wise, P. *Essential Endocrinology*. OUP, 1983. Chapter 5. (The Gonads.)

*MacKinnon, P.C.B. and Greenstein, B.D. 'Sexual Differentiation of the Brain'. In: *Human Growth* Vol. 2. Eds F. Falkner and J.M. Tanner. Plenum Publishing Corporation, New York, 1986.

*McGill, T.E. 'Genetic Factors Influencing the Action of Hormones on Sexual Behaviour'. In: *Biological Determinants of Sexual Behaviour*. Ed. J.B. Hutchison. John Wiley and Sons, Chichester, 1978.

Metropolitan Police. Performance Information Bureau. (Statistics on juvenile offenders to 1991.)

*Simpson, J.L. *Disorders of Sexual Differentiation*. Academic Press, New York, 1976.

Vega-Matuszczyk, J., Fernandez-Guasti, A. and Larsson, K. 'Sexual Orientation, Proceptivity, and Receptivity in the Male Rat as a Function of Neonatal Hormonal Manipulation'. Hormones and Behavior, 1988. 22, pp 362–378.

Wachtel, S.S. and Koo, G.C. 'H–Y antigen in Gonadal Differentiation'. In: *Mechanism of Sex Differentiation in Animals and Man*. Eds C.R. Austin and R.G. Edwards. Academic Press, London, 1981.

*Ward, I.L. 'The Prenatal Stress Syndrome: Current Status'. Psychoneuroendocrinology, 1984. 9, pp 3–11.

Chapter 4. Gene Shop

Beecher, M.D. and Beecher, I.M. 'Sociobiology of Bank Swallows: Reproductive Strategy of the Male'. Science, 1979. 205, pp 1282–1285.

*Betzig, L.L. *Despotism and Differential Reproduction: A Darwinian View of History.* Aldine, New York, 1986. (Dominant males get prettiest girls.)

Boone, J.L. III 'Parental Investment and Elite Family Structure in Preindustrial States: A Case Study of Late Medieval – Early Modern Portuguese Genealogies'. American Anthropologist, 1986. 88, pp 859–878. (Males seeking wealth.)

*Bourne, G.H. *The Ape People.* Rupert Hart Davies, London, 1971. (Naive male beaten up by female: squirrel, Drill monkey; humans tie stick to penis.)

Clutton-Brock, T.H. and Albon, S.D. 'The roaring of red deer and the evolution of honest advertisement.' Behaviour, 1979. 69, pp 145–170. (Red deer.)

*Cox, C.R. and LeBoeuf, B.J. 'Female Incitation of Male Competition: A Mechanism in Sexual Selection'. American Naturalist, 1977. 111, pp 317–335. (Female seal incites males to fight.)

Daly, M. & Wilson, M. 'Homicide and Kinship'. American Anthropologist, 1982. 84, pp 372–378. (Sexual jealousy and homicide.)

Davies, N.B. and Halliday, T.P. (1978). 'Deep croaks and fighting assessment in toads Bufo bufo.' Nature, 1978. 274, pp 683–685. (Toad's deep croaks.)

De Waal, F.B.M. 'Exploitative and familiarity-dependent support strategies in chimpanzees.' Behavior, 1978. 17, pp 268–312.

Duby, G. *The Chivalrous Society.* Transl. C. Poston.

Edward Arnold, London, 1977. pp 117–118. (French patriliny.)

*Dunbar, R.I.M. *Reproductive Decisions*. Princeton University Press, New Jersey, 1984. (Gelada baboons taking over a harem.)

Essock-Vitale, S.M. and McGuire, M.T. 'Women's Lives Viewed from an Evolutionary Perspective. I. Sexual Histories, Reproductive Success, and Demographic Characteristics of a random sam. of Am. wom.' Ethology and Sociobiology, 1985. 6, pp 137–154. (Reproductive success in U.S. women.)

Fiedler, K. 'Vergliegende verhaltensstudien an seenadein, Schlangennadeln und seepferdchen'. Zeitschrift für Tierpsychologie, 1954. 11, 358–416. (Sea horse.)

Galdikas, B.M.F. 'Orangutan Reproduction in the Wild'. In: *Reproductive Biology of The Great Apes*. Ed. C.E. Graham. Academic Press, New York, 1981. (Orang rape.)

Gladstone, D.E. 'Promiscuity in Monogamous Colonial Birds'. American Naturalist, 1979. 114, pp 545–557.

Groth, A.N. and Burgess, A.W. 'Rape: A Sexual Deviation'. American Journal of Orthopsychiatry, 1977. 47, pp 400–406. Married rapists.)

Guikes, F.W. *Norma Jean: The Life and Death of Marilyn Monroe*. Grafton, London, 1986.

Howard, R.D. 'Male Age-size Distribution and Male Mating Success in Bullfrogs'. In: *Natural Selection and Social Behavior*. Eds R.D. Alexander and D.W. Tinkle. Chiron, New York, 1981. (Sneak lovers.)

Kinsey, A.C., Pomeroy, W.B., Martin, C.E. and Gebhard, P.H. *Sexual Behavior in the Human Female*. Saunders, Philadelphia, 1953. (Women's preferences.)

Knodel, J. and Lynch, K.A. 'The Decline of Remarriage: Evidence from German Village Populations in the 18th and 19th Centuries'. Research report 84-57 of the Population Studies Center, University of Michigan, Ann Arbor, 1984. (Childless widow more likely to marry.)

Kruijt, J.P. and Hogan, J.A. 'Social Behavior of the Lek in Black Grouse. Lerutus tetrix tetrix (L.)'. Ardea, 1967. 55, pp 203–239. (Leks.)

Lehrman, D.S. 'Interaction between internal and external environments in the regulation of the reproductive cycle of the ring dove'. In: *Sex and Behavior*. Ed. F.A. Beach. Wiley, New York, 1965.

Liley, N.B. 'Ethological isolating mechanisms in four sympatric species of poeciliid fishes'. Behaviour, 1966. Supplement 13, 1–197. (Guppies.)

Lincoln, G.A. 'The Seasonal Reproductive Changes in the Red Deer Stag (Cervus elaphus)'. Journal of Zoology (London), 1971. 163, pp 105–123. (Seasonal breeding: red deer.)

Lloyd, J.E. 'Studies on the Flash Communication System in Photinus Fireflies'. Miscellaneous Publications of the Museum of Zoology, No. 130. Ann Arbor, University of Michigan, 1966. (Firefly flashes.)

Lockhard, J. and Adams, R.M. 'Human serial polygyny: Observational and Demographic Evidence'. Ethology and Sociobiology, 1981. 2, pp 177–186. (Older men and younger women.)

Noble, G.K. and Greenberg, B. 'Effects of seasons, castration and crystalline sex hormones upon the urogenital system and sexual behavior of the lizard Anolis carolinensis'. Journal of Experimental Zoology, 1941. 88, pp 451–479.

Rada, R.T., Kellner, R. and Winslow, W.W. 'Plasma Testosterone and Aggressive Behavior'. Psychosomatics, 1976. 17, pp 138–142. (Rapists and testosterone.)

Rijksen, H.D. *A Field Study on Sumatran Orang Utans*. H. Veenman and Zonen, B.V., Wageningen, 1978.

Smith, R.L. 'Paternity Assurance and Altered Roles in the Mating Behaviour of a Giant Water Bug. *Abedus herberti* (Heteroptera: Belosomatidae)'. Animal Behaviour, 1979. 27, pp 716–725. (Water bug.)

*Smuts, B.B. *Sex and Friendship in Baboons*. Aldine, New York, 1985. (Friendship among baboons.)

Sunday World, 1st June, 1986. (Samantha Fox.)

*Symons, D. *Play and Aggression: A Study of Rhesus Monkeys*. Columbia University Press, New York. pp 162–168. (Furtive behaviour.)

Thornhill, R. 'Sexual selection and nuptual feeding behavior in *Bittacus apicalis* (Insecta: Mecoptera)'. American Naturalist, 1976. 110, pp 529–548. (Hangingfly.)

Thornhill, R. & Alcock, J. *The Evolution of Insect Mating Systems*. Harvard University Press, Cambridge, Mass, 1983. (Insects and rape.)

*Thornhill, R. and Alcock, J. *The Evolution of Insect Mating Systems*. Harvard University Press, Cambridge, 1983. (Insects and rape.)

*Trivers, R.L. 'Parental Investment and Sexual Selection'. In: *Sexual Selection and the Descent of Man* 1871–1971. Ed. B. Campbell, Aldine, Chicago, 1972. (Parental investment.)

*Williams, G.C. *Sex and Evolution*. Princeton University Press, 1975. (Young women and fertility attraction.)

Wilson, E.O. *Sociobiology, the New Synthesis*. Harvard University Press, Cambridge, 1975. (Definition of competition.)

Wyre, R. and Swift, A. *Women, Men and Rape*. Hodder and Stoughton, Sevenoaks, 1990.

Chapter 5. Learning to be Superior

Beecher, M.D. and Beecher, I.M. 'Sociobiology of Bank Swallows: Reproductive Strategy of the Male'. Science, 1979. 205, pp 1282–1285. (Swallows, rape and cuckoldry.)

Baumgartner, A. ' "My Daddy might have Loved Me": Student Perceptions of Differences between Male and Female'. Institute for Equality of Education, Denver,

1983. (How boys see girlhood and vice versa.)

Condry, J. and Condry, S. 'Sex Differences in the Eye of the Beholder'. Child Development, 1976. 47, pp 812–819.

Erhardt, A.A. and Baker, S.W. 'Fetal Androgens, Human Central Nervous System Differentiation, and Behavior Sex Differences'. In: *Sex Differences in Behavior*. Eds R.C. Friedaman, R.M. Richart and R.L. Van de Wiele. Wiley, New York, 1974. (Congenital adrenal hyperplasia.)

Fagot, B.I. 'Consequences of Moderate Cross-gender Behavior in Pre-school Children'. Child Development, 1977. 48, pp 902–907. (Cross-gender behaviour.)

Ferri, E. 'Growing Up in a One-Parent Family'. National Foundation for Educational Research, Windsor, 1976. (Effects on education.)

Frisch, H.L. 'Sex Stereotypes in Adult–Infant Play'. Child Development, 1977. 48, pp 1671–1675.

Imber, M.J. 'Breeding Biology of the Grey-faced Petrel Pterodroma macroptera gouldi'. Ibis, 1976. 118, pp 51–64.

Fox, L.H. 'The Effects of Sex-role Socialization on Mathematics Participation and Achievement. Women and Mathematics: Research Perspectives for Change'. NIE Papers in Education and Work, 1977. No. 8. (Maths teachers are more likely to be men.)

Joffe, C. 'Sex Role Socialization and the Nursery School: As the Twig is Bent'. Journal of Marriage and the Family, 1971. 33, pp 467–475. (Sex type sterotyping in the nursery school.)

Kliemann, D.J. and Malcolm, J.R. 'The Evolution of Male Parental Investment in Mammals'. In: *Parental Care in Mammals*. Eds D.J. Gubernick and P.H. Klopfer. Plenum Press, 1981.

Kotelchuk, M. 'The Infant's Relationship to the Father: Experimental Evidence'. In: *The Role of the Father in Child Development*. Ed. M. Lamb. Wiley, New York, 1976.

Lambert, L. and Hart, S. 'Who Needs a Father?' New Society, 1978. 37, p 80.

Le Boef, B.J., Whiting, R.J. and Gantt, R.F. 'Perinatal Behavior of Northern Elephant Seal Families and their Young'. Behavior, 1972. 43, pp 121–156.

Lee, A.K., Bradley, A.J. and Braithwaite, R.W. 'Corticosteroid Levels and Male Mortality in Antechinus stuartii'. In: *The Biology of Marsupials*. Eds B. Stonehouse and D. Gilmore. University Park Press, Baltimore, 1977.

Lever J. 'Sex Differences in Games Children Play'. Social Problems, 1976. 23, pp 55–62.

Mack, J. 'Children Half-alone'. New Society, 1976. 38, pp 6–8. (Single-parent and child development.)

McKinney, F., Derrickson, S. and Mineau, P. 'Forced Copulation in Waterfowl'. Behavior, 1983. 86, pp 250–294. (Drake rape.)

Netboy, A. *The Columbia River Salmon and Steelhead Trout*. University of Washington Press, Seattle, 1980. (Salmon and semelparity.)

Parke, R.D. 'Perspectives on Father–Infant Interaction'. In: *Handbook of Infancy*. Ed. J.D. Osofsky. Wiley, New York, 1979.

*Pleck, J.H. *The Myth of Masculinity*. MIT Press, Cambridge, 1981. (Punishing boys who behave like girls.)

Power, H.W., Litowich, E. and Lombardo, M.P. 'Male Starlings Delay Incubation to Avoid Being Cuckolded'. Auk, 1981. 98, pp 386–389.

Rebelsky, F. and Hanks, C. 'Fathers' Verbal Interaction with Infants in the First Three Months of Life'. Child Development, 1971. 42, pp 63–68. (Fathers talk more to baby sons.)

Rendina, I. and Dickerscheid, J.D. 'Father Involvement with First-born Infants'. Family Coordinator, 1976. 25, pp 373–379. (Fathers talk more to baby boys.)

Rheingold, H. and Cook, K. 'The Contents of Boys' and Girls' Rooms as an Index of Parents' Behavior'. Child Development, 1975. 46, pp 459–463. (Child's toys chosen on basis of sex.)

Rubin, J.Z., Provenanzo, F. and Luria, Z. 'The Eye of the Beholder: Parents' Views on Sex of Newborns'. American Journal of Orthopsychiatry, 1974. 44, pp 512–519. (Girl babies look softer than boy babies.)

Serbin, L.A. and O'Leary, K.D. 'How Nursery Schools Teach Girls to Shut Up'. Psychology Today, 1975. 9, pp 56–58.(Boys get more attention in nursery class.)

Serbin, L.A., O'Leary, K.D., Kent, R.N. and Tonick, I.J. 'A Comparison of Teacher Response to the Pre-academic Problems and Problem Behavior of Boys and Girls'. Child Development, 1973. 44, pp 796–804. (Gender and nursery school play.)

Smith, C. and Lloyd, B.B. 'Maternal Behavior and Perceived Sex of Infant'. Child Development, 1978. 49, pp 1263–1266. (Mothers playing with disguised babies.)

*Tavris, C. and Wade, C. *The Longest War.* Harcourt Brace Jovanovich, San Diego, 1984. Chapter 6.

Chapter 6. Managing the Male

The Family Physician. Cassell & Company Ltd, London. Undated, but probably Victorian. (Nurses should be women.)

Statistical Abstracts of the USA (1982–3). Tables 231, 657.

Old Testament. Leviticus 27: 1–4. (Women should be paid less than men.)

*Bullough, V.L. *The Subordinate Sex.* Penguin, Baltimore, 1973. (Fénelon.)

Ellis, H. (1903). 'Variation in Man and Woman'. Popular Science Monthly, 1903. 62, pp 237–253.

Gauntlet, J. 'The spare sex'. Medical Laboratory World, November 1992. (Statistics on women in management.)

Terman, L.M. 'Mental and Physical Traits of a Thousand Gifted Children'. *Genetic Studies of Genius,* Vol. 1. Stanford University Press, California, 1925. Chapter 7.

Chapter 7. Crawling Under the Pipe Stem

Alexander, R.D., Hoogland, J.L., Noonan, K.M. and Sharman, P.W. 'Dimorphisms and Breeding Systems in Pinnipeds, Ungulates, Primates and Humans'. In: *Evolutionary Biology and Human Social Behavior. An Anthropological Perspective.* Eds N.A. Chagnon and W. Irons. Duxbury Press, Massachusetts, 1979. (Socially imposed monogamy.)

*Betelheim, B. *Symbolic Wounds*. Collier, New York, 1962. (Penis subincision.)

Fernea, E. and Fernea, R. 'A Look Behind the Veil'. Human Nature, 1979. 2, pp 69–80. (Purdah.)

Flinn, M.V. 'Parent–offspring Interactions in a Caribbean Village: Daughter Guarding.' In: *Human Reproductive Behavior. A Darwinian Perspective.* Eds L. Betzig, M. Borgerhoff Mulder and P. Turke. Cambridge University Press, 1988. (Trinidad – daughter guarding.)

Hadiyannakis, C. 'Les Tendences Contemporaines Concernant la répression du Délit d'Adultère'. Association Internationale de Droit Pénal, Thessalonika, 1969. (Adultery laws.)

*Hosken, F.P. 'The Hosken Report. Genital and Sexual Mutilation of Women'. 2nd Revised edition. Women's International Network News, Lexington, 1979. (Infibulation.)

Hunt, T. *Sexual Behavior in the 70s*. Playboy Press, Chicago, 1974. p 191.

*Jolly, A. *The Evolution of Primate Behavior*. 2nd Edition. MacMillan, New York, 1985. p 285. (Promiscuous female baboons.)

*Lederer, W. *The Fear of Women*. Harcourt Brace Jovanovich, New York, 1968.

*Lévi-Strauss, C. *The Elementary Structures of Kinship*. Beacon, Boston, 1969. (Bridewealth – a contract between men.)

Lott, D.F. 'Dominance Relations and Breeding Rate in Mature Male American Bison'. Zeitschrift für Tierpsychologie, 1979. 49, pp 418–432.

*Maccoby, E.E. and Jacklin, C.N. *The Psychology of Sex Differences*. Stanford University Press, Paolo Alto, 1974.

*Mead, M. *Sex and Temperament*. Dell, New York, 1963. (Couvade.)

Mulder, M.B. 'Kipsigis Bridewealth Payments'. In: *Human Reproductive Behavior. A Darwinian Perspective*. Eds L. Betzig, M.B. Mulder and P. Turke. Cambridge University Press, 1988.

Shepher, J. 'Mate Selection among Second Generation Kibbutz Adolescents and Adults: Incest Avoidance and Negative Imprinting'. Archives of Sexual Behavior, 1971. 1, pp 293–307.

Short, R.V. 'The Origins of Sexuality'. In: *Reproduction in Mammals*, Vol. 8: Human Sexuality. Eds C.R. Austin and R.V. Short. Cambridge University Press, 1980. (Polygyny.)

*Spiro, M.E. *Children of the Kibbutz*. Harvard University Press, Cambridge, 1958.

*Tavris, C. and Wade, C. *The Longest War*. Harcourt Brace Jovanovich, San Diego, 1984. Chapter 7.

*Wagner, G. *The Bantu of North Kavirondo* Vol. 1. Oxford University Press, 1949.

Yom-Tov, Y. 'Intraspecific Nest Parasitism in Birds'. Biological Reviews, 1980. 55, pp 93–108. (Cuckolded starlings.)

Chapter 8. The Male in Court

*Patemen, Carole. *The Sexual Contract*. Polity Press, Oxford, 1988.

Treitel, G.H. *The Law of Contract*. 7th Edition. Sweet and Maxwell Ltd, London, 1987. pp 336, 337, 490, 491.

Chapter 9. Sex For Sale

Beauvoir, Simone de. *The Second Sex.* Translated and edited by H.M. Parsnley. Knopf, New York, 1953.

Jennings, M.A. 'The Victim as Criminal: A Consideration of California's Criminal Law'. California Review, 1976. 64, pp 1251. (Prostitution in U.S.)

Johnson, A.M., Wadsworth, J., Wellings, K., Bradshaw, S. and Field, J. 'Sexual Lifestyles and HIV Risk'. Nature, 1992. 360, pp 410–412.

McLeod, E. *Women Working: Prostitution Now.* Croom Helm, London, 1982. pp 12–13. (Prostitution in Birmingham, UK.)

San Francisco Examiner, 3 February, 1985. (Prostitution and money in U.S.)

Chapter 10. Man To Man

*Ardrey, R. *The Territorial Imperative: A Personal Enquiry into the Animal Origins of Property and Nations.* Atheneum, New York, 1966. (Male bonding – property and power.)

Boswell, J. 'Revolutions, Universals and Sexual Categories'. In: *Hidden From Memory: Reclaiming the Gay and Lesbian Past.* Eds M. Duberman, M. Vicinus and G. Chauncey, Jr. Penguin, London, 1989. (Homosexuality – categorization.)

Brown, N.B. 'Inquiry into the Feminine Mind'. New York Times Magazine, 12 April, 1964. (Male bonding – women voters follow men.)

Bullough, V.R. *Sexual Variance in Society and History.* University of Chicago Press, 1976. (Homosexuality during the Renaissance.)

de Vore, I. and Hall, K.R.L. 'Baboon Social Behavior'. In: *Primate Behavior: Field Studies of Monkeys and Apes.* Ed. I. de Vore. Hold, Rheinhart and Winston, New York, 1965. (Male bonding and apes.)

Faderman, L. *Surpassing the Love of Men.* Morrow, New York, 1981. (Lesbianism – history.)

Hunt, T. 'Australian Women'. Australian Quarterly, 1963. 35, p 80. (Australian women MPs.)

Montague, A. *The Nature of Human Aggression.* Oxford University Press, 1976. p 186. (Tahiti.)

Tiger, L. *Men In Groups.* Marion Boyars, New York, 1984. (Male bonding as biological imperative.)

Wilkinson, R. *The Prefects: British Leadership and the Public School Tradition.* Oxford University Press, 1964. (Male bonding and party unity.)

Chapter 11. Hawks and Doves

Maynard Smith, J. *Evolution and the Theory of Games.* Cambridge University Press, 1991.

Chapter 12. One Less War

Blurton Jones, N.G. and Kanner, M.J. 'Sex Differences in the Behaviour of London and Bushmen Children'. In: *Comparative Ecology and Behaviour of Primates.* Eds R.P. Michael and J.H. Crooks. Academic Press, London, 1973. (Kalahari children.)

Campbell, A. 'Female Aggression'. In: *Aggression and Violence.* Eds P. Marsh and A. Campbell. Basil Blackwell, Oxford, 1982. (Girls becoming violent.)

Depp, F.C. 'Violent Behavior Patterns on Psychiatric Wards'. Aggressive Behavior, 1976. 2, pp 295–306. (Psychiatric wards and male aggression.)

*Gelles, R.J. *The Violent Home.* Gage, California, 1972. (Wifebeating – from father to son.)

Hamilton, Edith. *Mythology.* Mentor Books, New York, 1942.

*Henley, N.M. *Body Politics, Power, Sex, and Non-Verbal Behavior.* Prentice-Hall, New Jersey, 1977. (Male–female expressions.)

Lyndon, N. 'Badmouthing'. Sunday Times Magazine, 9 December, 1990.

Maccoby, E.E. and Jacklin, C.N. 'Sex Differences in Aggression: A Rejoinder and a Reprise'. Child Development, 1980. 51, pp 964–980. (Boys play rougher than girls.)

*Money, J. and Erhard, A.A. *Man, Woman, Boy and Girl.* John Hopkins University Press, Baltimore, 1972. (Girls, aggression and prenatal testosterone and progesterone.)

Mazur, A. and Lamb, T.A. 'Testosterone, Status and Mood in Modern Males'. Hormones and Behavior, 1980. 14, pp 236–246. (Tennis and testosterone.)

Miles, R. *The Rites of Man.* Grafton Books, London, 1991.

Reinisch, J.M. 'Prenatal Exposure to Synthetic Progestins Increases Potential for Aggression in Humans'. Science, 1981. 211, pp 1171–1173.

*Rogers, S.C. 'Woman's place: a Critical Review of Anthropological Theory'. Comparative Studies in Society and History, 1978. 20, pp 123–162. (Differentials.)

Rose, R.M., Gordon, T.P. and Bernstein, I.S. 'Plasma Testosterone Levels in Male Rhesus: Influences of Sexual and Social Stimuli'. Science, 1972. 178, pp 643–645. (Defeat and low testosterone.)

Oetzel, R.M. 'Annotated Bibliography'. In: *The Development of Sex Differences.* Ed. E.E. Maccoby. Stanford University Press, California, 1966. (Boys play rougher than girls.)

Rosenblatt, P.C. *Grief and Mourning in Cross-Cultural Perspective.* Human Relations Area File Press, New Haven, 1976.

Roy, M. 'A Survey of 150 Cases'. In: *Battered Women: A Psychological Study of Domestic Violence.* Ed. M. Roy. Van Nostrand, New York, 1977. (Wifebeating: New York police.)

Rubenstein, C. 'Wellness in All'. Psychology Today, October 1982. 16, pp 28–38. (Males, work and heart disease.)

*Smith, J. *Misogynies*. Faber and Faber Ltd., London, 1989.

Social Trends: 1977, 1979, 1984. Central Statistics Office. H.M. Stationery Office, London, nos. 8, 9, 14. (Crimes of violence and men.)

Men, Masculinities & Social Theory. Eds J. Hearn and David Morgan. Unwin Hyman, London, 1990.

Taylor, E.B. *Primitive Culture*. Vol. 1, London, 1871. p 2.

Index